What Have the Germans Ever Done For Us?

Susan Duxbury-Neumann

AMBERLEY

ACKNOWLEDGMENTS AND COPYRIGHT INFORMATION

The author and publisher would like to thank the following people/organisations for permission to use copyright material in this book:

Karl-Heinz Wüstner: Text taken from – *New Light on the German Pork Butchers in Britain (1850-1950)*.
Margaret & Michael Grace, Beaconsfield & District Historical Society (The White House at Wilton Park).
Paul Raftery, Photographer, Hants, UK – Image of the Roskilde Viking ship.
The Baring Archive, London (portrait of John Baring of Larkbear by William Hoare).
German Emigration Center, Bremerhaven – *The Poor Palatines*.
Eileen Haffner at George Haffner (Foods) Ltd – image of German Pork Butcher's Shop.
Alamy – Invoice number IY00596420 – Sugar making at the Counterslip refinery, Bristol.

Every attempt has been made to seek permission for copyright material used in this book. However, if we have inadvertently used copyright material without permission/acknowledgement we apologise and we will make the necessary correction at the first opportunity.

First published 2017

Amberley Publishing
The Hill, Stroud
Gloucestershire, GL5 4EP

www.amberley-books.com

British Library Cataloguing in Publication Data.
A catalogue record for this book is available from the British Library.

ISBN 978 1 4456 6486 6 (print)
ISBN 978 1 4456 6487 3 (ebook)

Typeset in 9.5pt on 11.5pt Sabon.
Origination by Amberley Publishing.
Printed in the UK.

CONTENTS

1

Who Are The Germans?

During the Roman occupation of Europe, which came to an end in the fifth century AD, numerous German-speaking countries were among the hundreds of multi-ethnic independent kingdoms of The Holy Roman Empire governed by kings, dukes, counts, bishops, abbots and other rulers collectively known as 'princes'. Throughout the medieval and early modern periods, this complex of territories has played a fundamental role in central European history.

When the Romans began their withdrawal from Britain in the early fifth century, so too did the source of any major written historical data. However, although the *Anglo-Saxon Chronicle* – one of the most important documents that has come down to us from the Middle Ages – might not be completely accurate[1], it helps to give a clearer insight into what actually happened in Britain 1,000 years ago.

Historical and scientific research along with widespread excavation has proved that many fierce battles were fought between Britons and Anglo-Saxons during the fifth and early sixth centuries, which is one reason why this period of history has become known as the 'Dark Age'. Even though Britain no longer had the strong Roman army to defend it from warring and raiding invaders, those who entered Britain between the sixth and eleventh centuries founded what was to become Britain. These were mostly Germanic tribes of the Holy Roman Empire – Goths, Angles, Saxons, Lombards, Frisians and Franks.

The most lasting influence of European culture in Britain is the English language, which has its roots in the Germanic languages of mainland Europe. Apart from the Angles, after whom English is named, this also includes the Netherlands and Denmark. Many everyday words in English are of Germanic origin, while more intellectual and formal words originate from French, Latin and Greek. English is not the only significant native language spoken in Britain today – others are Gaelic and Welsh – and German is not the only native language spoken in Germany – others are Lower Sorbian and Upper Sorbian, spoken by a Slavic minority in the Lusation region of eastern Germany. Nevertheless, the shared origins of English and German – both their language and culture – are undeniable.

But the degree of genetic heritage connecting Britain and Germany has been more difficult to measure. The first detailed study of the genetics of British people has revealed that the Romans, Vikings and Normans may have ruled or invaded the British for hundreds of years, but left barely a trace on our DNA. The analysis shows that the Anglo-Saxons were the only conquering force around AD 400–500 to substantially alter the country's genetic makeup, with most white British people now owing almost 30 per cent of their DNA to the ancestors of modern-day Germans.[2] Reinforced by studies on a segment of the Y-chromosome of almost all Danish and northern German men found

The Coppergate or York Anglo Saxon Helmet, dated between AD 700–820 – the most outstanding example of the Anglo-Saxon period to survive in Europe.

On the crest is an inscription in Latin that translates as, 'In the name of our Lord Jesus Christ, the Holy Spirit and God; and to all we say amen. Oshere'. Oshere was probably the name of its owner, possibly of the Northumbrian Royal Dynasty. (Image courtesy of York Museums Trust – public domain).

to be surprisingly common in Great Britain, it has now become clear that the nation that most disliked the Germans were once Germans themselves.[3]

Historians are uncertain when Anglo-Saxons from the coastal regions of Germany began entering Britain, although the *Anglo-Saxon Chronicle* records a group of West-Saxons as having entered Britain in three ships at 'the place that is called Cerdic's-Ore' in AD 514. Archaeological findings also suggest that groups of Anglo-Saxons occupied smaller areas of the country, having previously served as mercenary soldiers with the Roman army. Later, they were attracted by Britain's rich farmland. The flat, marshy, coastal landscape of their north German homeland was prone to regular flooding, destroying their animals, crops and settlements along a rapidly changing coastline. Archaeologists suspect that 'up to 200,000 emigrants' as whole families crossed the North Sea in small boats looking for new places to settle; usually in the spring and summer when the sea was calm. Their ships bulged with household goods, tools, weapons and even farm animals.[4] The rich countryside and easily navigable rivers of eastern Britain must have proved very welcoming to emigrating Angles, who left their former homeland massively depopulated, according to the *Chronicle*'s written recordings. The Angles from the areas around northern Germany settled in eastern parts of Britain; the Saxons settled further south, hence the name Anglo-Saxons, which included the North German Frisians who quickly established control over modern-day England.[5]

The first Anglo-Saxon king and dominant ruler in England was Alfred the Great (849–899), who successfully defended his kingdom against Viking attempts at conquest. The Vikings, who were fearsome Germanic Norse seafarers, began entering Britain in the late eighth century, primarily to raid and pillage monasteries. After a period of unrest, they began trading from their Scandinavian homelands (part of which is now Denmark and northern Germany) across wide areas of northern, central and Eastern Europe and as far as Central Asia. Between the eighth and late eleventh centuries they became the

This is the largest Viking ship ever discovered; 37 meters long and carefully reconstructed after 1,000 years languishing beneath the Roskilde Fjord in Denmark, it is currently on display at the British Museum in London. (© Paul Raftery / Rogers, Stirk Harbour and Partners).

first traders of any significance – international tradesmen of their time – to enter central areas of Britain by sailing upstream in their longships.

Viking traders bought goods and materials such as silver, silk, spices, wine, jewellery, glass and pottery. In return they sold items such as honey, tin, wheat, wool, wood, iron, fur, leather, fish and walrus ivory, as well as buying and selling slaves. Traders carried folding scales for weighing coins to make sure they got a fair deal. In Ireland they founded the city of Dublin and in England they made the town of York the most important trading town outside of London.

Extensive and detailed excavation have revealed houses, workshops and backyards of the Viking city of Jorvik on the site where it stood, in north England's city of York, nearly 1,000 years ago. Similarly, the Viking settlement of Haithabu on the Schlei River near the historical north German town of Schleswig (which had strong trading-connections with Jorvik) has also been reconstructed on the site of a functioning trading-post, giving visitors an authentic insight into Viking traditions.

Besides the merchants, during the early Middle Ages smaller independent colonies of Vikings began settling in Britain as farmers, as well as skilful craft workers, highly competent boat builders, and sailors. In the following chapters, we can examine the steady and continuous flow of migration from Germany to Britain from the early Middle Ages until the first half of the twentieth century.

2

EARLY TRANS-MIGRATION

The Merchants

Following the Viking traders and earlier settlers, from the Middle Ages onwards, German merchants, attracted by a liberal immigration policy, began entering Britain. Encouraged by Henry II, who in 1157 bestowed them with privileges with the intention of attracting foreigners with superior skills and knowledge, their numbers grew steadily. Merchants from Cologne, the North Sea, and Baltic areas played an important part in supplying the rapidly growing British population with merchandise, as well as trading local produce at markets and fairs. Tin, wool and later cloth were the main goods the Germans exported from ports in England and Scotland, in exchange for a wide variety of merchandise from Germany, Italy and the Netherlands.[1] By 1300, north German seafaring merchants based in Hamburg and Lübeck had formed a commercial and defensive confederation of merchant guilds known as the Hanseatic League. The League consisted of affluent trading points along the North and Baltic Sea routes, created to protect economic interests and diplomatic privileges in affiliated cities and countries with its own legal system and armies for mutual protection and aid. Up to 200 towns and cities in northern Europe were members of the League, as were several large trading houses. Some of them still exist today in Germany and are known as the Hanse or Hansa. It was chiefly through the enterprise of these first 'trans-migrants' that early trade began to develop in Britain and became a vital component to the British economy.

From 1250 onwards Hansa merchants occupied their own enclave at the 'Steelyard' in London, to take advantage of the rich opportunities England had to offer. It was chiefly through their enterprise that London became one of the world's leading trading centres. Founded on the riverside, near Cosin Lane, now Ironbridge Wharf, it grew into a virtual micro-state on the banks of the Thames in the City of London where the merchants lived in austere seclusion, forbidden to marry native women or admit them to the premises.[2]

The Steelyard, like other Hansa stations throughout Europe, was a separate walled community with its own river warehouses, weighing house, chapel, counting houses, residential quarters, and aldermen, as well as a guildhall.[3]

By the mid-fourteenth century, the Hanse had gained control of all known trade-routes in the northern hemisphere, including the lucrative Russian markets, which dealt in furs, wax and honey, timber, and especially Herring, which was in great demand during periods of religious fasting. Travelling the East–West route, the Hansa obtained fine materials from Flanders, metal goods such as weapons, nails and wires, and also wine from France and Spain. In their sturdy and fast-moving cog-built vessels, which could carry up to 200 tons and were specially constructed with fore-and stern-castles as a defence against pirates, they were able to cross even the most dangerous passages.[4]

The Hanse merchant Georg Gisze (1497–1562) was born in Danzig in 1497 as the son of an alderman. As a member of the Hanseatic League, Georg was stationed in the 1530s at the London branch of the Hanse, the 'Steelyard'. The members of the Steelyard sat for a famous series of portraits by Hans Holbein the Younger.

A Latin couplet above the merchant's head suggests how faithfully the artist has rendered every aspect of the man: 'What you see here, this picture, shows Georg's features and figure such is his eye in real life, such is the shape of his cheeks.'

The portrait identifies him by his clothing and instruments as a merchant. On the table is a pewter writing stand with goose feathers, ink, sand, wax disks and sealing wax. Beside it are scissors, a signet ring and a seal. Near the table's edge, in the centre foreground, stands a small table clock which, together with the fragile Venetian glass vase and the perishable flowers, is a reminder of the passage of time. The carnations in the glass were a sign of betrothal in the medieval language of symbols.

The name Georg Gisze appears several times in various styles of handwriting on the documents attached to the wall. The letter he is holding suggests he has been corresponding with a brother in Germany, written in Middle Saxon. The plaque depicted over his head states that he is in his thirty-fourth year, in 1532. (© National Museums in Berlin through bpk-bildgentur).

The mid-seventeenth century brought the decline of the Hansa in Britain, its merchants being in direct competition with those of the City of London causing great hostility among British merchants. Most of its buildings were destroyed during the Great Fire of London in 1666.[5]

The Refugees

Martin Luther (1483–1546) was a German theologian and one of the most influential personas in European history. He introduced the Protestant Reformation in his 'Ninety-five Theses', which objected to teachings and practices of the late-medieval Catholic Church. Many historians claim this to have triggered the Thirty Years' War, which began in 1618 as a clash between the Protestant and Catholic states of the Holy Roman Empire.

The war developed into an all-out conflict involving most European countries and is known to have been one of the most destructive combats in European history. It saw the devastation of entire regions, bringing famine and disease to almost half the population of central Europe and, by the end of the war in 1648, most of the combatant powers were bankrupt and unable to fund their armies. This resulted in further looting and plundering by mercenaries and soldiers. So great was the destruction that some regions, for example Württemberg, lost three quarters of its population; Brandenburg lost half and in some areas an estimated two thirds of the population died. The male population of the German states was reduced by almost half.[6]

The end of the Thirty Year's War brought no lasting peace to Europe; instead, it had destabilised the whole region. Conflicts between neighbouring states served the interests of rulers, monarchs, and despots eager to enlarge their territories and strengthen

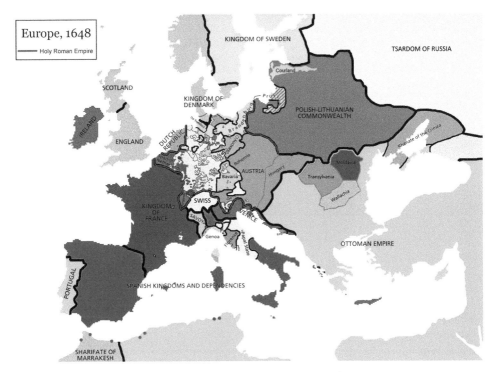

Map of Europe 1648 – the red line marks the border of the Holy Roman Empire. (Penguin atlas of modern history; GNU Free Documentation License).

their power. It is no wonder that by the end of the seventeenth century these hundreds of German states had failed to achieve economic recovery in comparison with other neighbouring principalities. The Netherlands' economy, for example, was already expanding rapidly by the beginning of the Industrial Revolution.[7]

During this period of history, German economic growth was also hampered by narrow-minded officialdom. The strict boundaries and complicated tax laws of the almost 500 micro-states hampered regional development causing widespread unrest. The abolishment of serfdom, allowing wealthy peasants to own most of the formal land, introduced the German laws of primogeniture. This granted permission for only one son in a family to inherit his fathers' land; a strong motivation for many young Germans to leave their home for a new country where they could hope to own their land and prosper with minimal government hindrance.[8]

Contrary to Germany's development, the religious wars on the continent supported Britain's economic immigration policy to an unforeseen degree. With the help of refugees fleeing religious persecution, Britain was transformed from an economically backward country to one on the verge of becoming the world's first industrial and commercial power. In 1709 Parliament passed a new liberal naturalisation Act with the explicit intention of attracting foreigners. The Act omitted any stipulations regarding educational, occupational or property provisions, as the immigration of poverty-stricken foreigners was unthinkable at that time. This would very soon prove itself to be a fateful error of judgement.

Towards the end of the seventeenth and into the eighteenth century, the previously wealthy region of the Middle Rhine area of the Holy Roman Empire known as 'The County Palatine of the Rhine' had been repeatedly invaded by French troops, resulting in continuous military requisitions and widespread devastation and famine. Higher taxation was only one of the destructive aftereffects of war; a particularly cold winter destroyed vines, fruit trees and crops, rendering peasants and farmers destitute, forcing them to leave their land and search for a better life elsewhere. On the instigation of Britain's Queen Anne, who during her reign from 1702 until 1714 had advertised for workers in the British/American colony of Carolina, the Palatines came to Britain having been promised a ship's passage to the New World and, furthermore, free land in the American colonies.[9]

Such was their situation when large groups of Palatines arrived in London between May and November 1709; fleeing religeous persecution by the thousand, having travelled down the Rhine River to the Dutch city of Rotterdam before embarking for London. The first boats packed with German Palatines landed in May 1709. Throughout the summer, ships unloaded thousands of refugees. Altogether, 16,000 Roman Catholic Palatines (from an area known today as the Pfälz) arrived in London, completely overwhelming initial attempts by British authorities to provide for them.

By summer most of the 'Poor Palatines' had settled in army tents erected on the London fields of Blackheath and Camberwell. A committee dedicated to coordinating their settlement and dispersal sought ideas for their employment; this proved difficult, the Palatines being unskilled rural labourers who were neither sufficiently educated nor healthy enough for most types of employment. Now it seemed that these bedraggled and destitute migrants were hopelessly stranded in London, having spent the little money they had on their journey to Britain. 'The poor Palatines' became a synonym for German migrants who in general were welcomed by the British – but not 16,000 at once.[10]

The famous author Daniel Defoe posed the question 'What shall we do with them?' in his monthly 'Review of the State of the British Nation'. He analysed their situation and offered various solutions to the problems confronting the British government. Although

Accommodating the 'Poor Palatines' in tents on Blackheath; London, 1709. (© Sammlung Deutsches Auswandererhaus).

many people were willing to donate food and clothing, unhygienic conditions resulted in disease and a high death toll, which was also caused by violence and animosity shown by thugs and villains towards these poor, uneducated, and helpless peasants. The British government decided to solve the problem by refusing further entry into the country.

Since the British monarchy had broken with the Catholic church, it was ruled that migrants of the Roman Catholic faith must either convert or return to their homeland. Around 4,000 Catholics faced repatriation on the Continent.

Simultaneously, and supported by Queen Anne of England, landlords of Irish estates decided to increase their Protestant tenant population. In September 1709, almost 3,000 Palatines were relocated to rural Ireland, although during the following three years around two thirds of the Irish Palatine settlers left Ireland and returned to England and Germany.

Of the landlords who successfully managed to induce their allotment of Palatine immigrants to remain in rural Ireland, the most successful was Sir Thomas Southwell of Castle Matrix near Rathkeale, Co. Limerick. He championed the Palatines to secure government support for the settlement venture and took care of many of their initial needs at considerable personal expense, being reimbursed only just before his death in 1720. In 1711 Southwell had retained only ten families, but by 1714 settled about 130 families on his lands. The region around his demesne has retained the largest concentration of Irish Palatine residents to this day, having made innovative contributions to Irish farming life and the development of world Methodism, in Killeheen, Ballingrane, and Courtmatrix.[11]

In the summer of 1710 the British government organised the transportation of 3,000 German Palatines to New York and 600 to North Carolina in ten ships – the largest group of immigrants to enter the colony before the American Revolution, arriving on ships sponsored by the British government. Because of their refugee status and weakened condition, as well as shipboard diseases, they suffered a high rate of fatality during their journey. Having reached the New World, despite unfulfilled promises of land and regardless of being assigned to pay off their passages in work camps situated along the Hudson River, they were determined to stay.

From the original number of Palatines entering Britain, about 250 families remained in England; some weavers settled in Bolton and others found employment with the Liverpool Corporation.[12] Unfortunately, this sudden influx of poor and destitute migrants from the Palatinate who had arrived in Britain only weeks after the passing of the 1709 Parliament Liberal Naturalization Act represented a disastrous blow to Britain's liberal immigration policy. It was abolished three years later and no further immigration laws were passed in the aftermath of the Palatines' arrival.[13]

As with the Palatines and from the beginning of the eighteenth century onwards, thousands of German peasants left their homes for the New World. A smaller minority came to Britain, many of whom settled in London. In 1750, England had a population of approximately 5.74 million (in 2015 around 65 million), having regained a similar level prior to the mortality crisis of the fourteenth century caused by the Black Death or the Bubonic Plague, which is said to have killed 60 per cent of Europe's population alongside wars and a disruption of food supplies. Before 1815 only fragmentary statistics record the number of British citizens who left the country as being around 20,000 persons.

German migrants on their way across the Atlantic to the New World travelled via England. Some arrived in England against their will, as recorded in the writings of Johann Wilhelm von Archenholtz in his essays, 'A Picture of England in 1797':

> An extraordinary event, which occurred a few years since, will serve to elucidate the noble and generous manner of thinking among the English. The emigrations from the Empire, of which such sad complaints are made, even at this day, and which are founded on reasons partly just, and partly imaginary, gave opportunity to a German gentleman to form a very singular scheme. The name of this projector and his intentions are still unknown; the arts which he practised to put to execution such a well concerted plan, are equally obscure. In the year 1765 he went to London at the head of 800 adventurers (emigrants) consisting of men, women and children, whom he had collected in the Palatinate, in Franconia, and in Swabia by promising them they would be much more happy in the British colonies.
>
> On their arrival at the port of London, this singular man disappeared, and has never since been heard of. At once miserable and disappointed, these unfortunate wretches, neither knowing the language nor being acquainted with any of the inhabitants, and with only a few rags to cover them, were entirely bewildered in that extensive capital. Without an asylum, without even bread for their children, who asked for it with the most piercing cries, they knew not to whom they could address themselves...

Dr Wachsel of the German Lutheran Church in London heard of their plight. He discovered them to be without food and shelter, some having already died of starvation, and resolved to advertise this singular event in the newspaper. The article describes the generous sums of money donated throughout the following weeks; enough to pay their passages to North America. On their arrival in Carolina they received the rest of the money to support a new start.

From the 1840s most German migrants sailed from Hamburg to east-coast British ports and then travelled by rail to Liverpool, from where they continued their journey to America – Liverpool being the main port of departure for thousands of people seeking new lives in the New World. Before embarking, many faced exploitation in overfilled boarding houses; some found work in London and decided to remain, partly because they did not have enough money to continue their trip. Many were victims of fraudulent ship's captains and there were reports of them sleeping in warehouses and 'labouring under illness'. According to a letter from the Society of Friends of Foreigners in Distress, which supported all foreigners in Britain, hundreds of emigrants who had made their way to London during the 1830s in the hope of securing a ship to the USA had found themselves stranded for several years after.[14]

In 1844 alone, almost 3,000 German sailors landed in Hull on 274 different ships, which brought further development to German communities along Britain's east coast. The largest German community outside London, however, was Liverpool, where sailors also contributed to its growth. They formed a large proportion of its revolving society with a daily number of approximately 250 German sailors on land. Although between 1820 and 1920 around five million people emigrated to the United States and other Commonwealth countries, a comparative few preferred to remain nearer home and take the shorter and less dangerous journey to Britain. Therefore, one might argue, those who left Britain were replaced by those who entered the country in search of a better life. Certainly, throughout the nineteenth century, the British government's restrictions on people entering the country was extremely lenient and of little concern; alternatively, Britain had become a major exporter of people to the British colonies and America. Between 1826 and 1848 and 1850 and 1905, there were no laws that could be used to prevent aliens from entering the country. In addition, it was easy for non-British subjects to set up in business and there was, indeed, a need in Britain for enterprising overseas merchants. In many cases chain migration developed as a result of letters describing successful business ventures and luxurious living conditions, giving the impression that in 'rich England money lies on the street'.[15] This formed close-knit communities of families and social contacts in certain professional networks, as described in the following chapters.

The growing Empire created an increasing demand for people who could organize supplies for its colonies and the re-export of colonial comodities. Britain lacked natural resources and became dependent on the import of raw and semi-finished products for its colonies as well as for the navy and industry. Markets also had to be found for colonial products that could not be consumed in Britain. In order to encourage economic development, Britain established – besides providing favourable economic and legal conditions – a military, financial and fiscal framework to provide advantageous circumstances for enterprising merchants and entrepreneurs. A 'rags-to-riches' career, usually associated with America, was also possible in eighteenth and nineteenth century Britain.[16]

Until Napoleon's dissolution of the Holy Roman Empire in 1806, and at no time previously during its long history, had the German-speaking states possessed clearly defined boundaries. In 1756 the famous French writer Voltaire fittingly described it as, 'This agglomeration which was called and which still calls itself the Holy Roman Empire was neither holy, nor Roman, nor an Empire'.

The 'Rheinbund' formed in 1806 had lasted only nine years, consisting of sixteen southern German states governed by Napoleon until his defeat in 1815. Following that, the consolidation of Germany took place in Venice and became known as 'The German Confederation'. This consisted of a loose association of thirty-nine German-speaking states in Central Europe and lasted until 1866. Germany was then without a central government but dominated by Austria and Prussia. This was intended to coordinate German-speaking countries replacing the former Holy Roman Empire.

Map of Confederation of the Rhine 1812 by Ziegelbrenner; Putzger – Historischer Weltatlas, 89. Auflage, 1965. (© GNU Free Documentation License).

To understand the reason for migration between Germany and Britain during the first half of the nineteenth century (whereby the German community in Britain far outnumbered its British counterpart in Germany) we should examine the German economy after the creation of The German Confederation, which had the intention of bringing peace and political reform to central Europe. Germany's lower classes – farmers, artisans, and factory workers – were not included in Confederation discussions concerning political and economic reform. Although farmers had been freed to some degree of their many obligations and dues owed to the landowning aristocracy, they were still often desperately poor and earned barely enough to survive. Farmers west of the Elbe River usually had properties too small to yield any kind of prosperity. Farmers east of the Elbe had become landless labourers hired to work on large estates.

Artisans who were skilled workers in handicrafts and trades and who belonged to the traditional guilds saw their economic position worsen as a result of industrialisation, which began to appear in Germany around 1815. As in Britain, the guilds attempted to stop factory construction and unrestricted commerce, but strong economic trends ran counter to their wishes. Therefore, in comparison to other European countries and because development was hindered by the abundance of autonomic territories, agriculture still dominated the German economy until the second half of the century. By 1850 wage earners amounted to only 20 per cent of the total workforce; crop failure and continuing conflict was still forcing thousands of small-holding farmers and peasants into migration. Furthermore, the conflict between the two dominant states of the German Confederation – Austria and Prussia – about who had the inherent right to rule German lands, had ended in favour of Prussia after the Austro-Prussian War in 1866. This resulted in the collapse of the Confederation and, later, the creation of the new German Empire.[17]

According to the 1861 census, the number of Germans in Britain was recorded at 28,644, and by 1891 had risen to 50,599, whereby half of those entering the country had settled in London.[18] Attracted by this well-established German colony, poorer migrants would, as in earlier years, often disembark at Hull or Liverpool to look for work and replenish their funds before continuing their travels – or were told by a dishonest captain that they had landed in America and could be seen wandering the streets in search of food and shelter.[19] Many Germans who had already set up in business were notorious for taking advantage of a poor migrant's misfortune. Having given them a job they paid outrageously low wages, which induced further poverty. This was the cause of a great deal of protest and government upheaval, which finally led to the tightening of the newly established Aliens Act of 1905, designed to prevent paupers or criminals from entering the country.

3

GERMAN CONTRIBUTION TOWARDS BRITAIN'S ECONOMIC GROWTH

The invention of the printing press by the German Johannes Gutenberg around 1440 should be classed as one of the greatest events in world history. It caused a revolution in the development of both culture and commerce equalled by hardly any other incident in the Christian era.

Gutenberg, a goldsmith by profession, developed a complete printing system based on existing screw presses originally used by the Romans as wine and oil presses. He perfected the printing process by adapting existing technologies as well as making his own groundbreaking inventions; this included the development of the beautiful calligraphy found in the books of the fifteenth century. *The Gutenberg Bible*, printed by Johannes Gutenberg in Mainz, Germany in the 1450s, marked the beginning of the printing revolution, being the first major book printed using movable metal type. It is written in Latin and has an iconic status, being widely praised for its high aesthetic and artistic qualities. Since its publication, forty-nine copies have survived and are considered to be among the most valuable books in the world.

The printing press spread within several decades to over 200 cities in a dozen European countries. By 1500 printing presses in operation throughout Western Europe had already produced more than twenty million volumes. In the sixteenth century, with presses spreading further afield, their output grew to an estimated 150 to 200 million copies. The operation of a press became so synonymous with the enterprise of printing that it lent its name to an entire new branch of media – 'the Press'. Printing has not only been the basis of cultural development and industrial growth, but has been an indispensable factor in the education of people at large.

The Navigation Acts, which were not abolished until 1857, were an obstacle to the use of German-owned shipping when trading with England. Shipping was controlled under the British flag with the intention of tightening government management of trade between England, its colonies and the rest of the world. Therefore, foreign merchants who wished to trade with countries belonging to the British Empire, not only had to settle in Britain but also acquire British nationality with the result that many German merchants settled in Britain. This was greatly encouraged by the British government, who preferred to see foreign overseas merchants and skilled workers with rare or superior qualities entering the country, rather than poverty-stricken foreigners such as the destitute migrants from the Palatinate.

The port of Hull served the Midlands and large industrial towns such as Leeds, Bradford and Sheffield, which maintained good trade relations with Hamburg and the

IMPRESSIO LIBRORVM.

Potest vt vna vox capi aure plurima: Linunt ita vna scripta mille paginas.

The Gutenberg Press. This engraving of the printing process, by Theodor Galle, is based on an earlier work – *Nova Reperta* ('New Discoveries') by Stradanus (also known as Jan van der Straet) – and illustrates the various steps of printing. (Image online, courtesy of the Library of Congress).

Baltic ports. Even so, London remained the most important port for Hamburg's trade with England. In the eighteenth century merchant houses in London often worked in partnership with two to four traders. Capital would be given partly by credit on inheritance by well-meaning parents or godparents, or provided through the family network of established European merchant houses with worldwide connections.[1]

By the beginning of the eighteenth century this influx of knowledgeable and enterprising migrants had transformed Britain from an economically backward country into the first industrial and commercial world power. Not only was their knowledge of international business and their many overseas connections proving an advantage to British trading abroad, they, in turn, were able to access new markets, especially in the British colonies. Therefore, Britain's liberal immigration policy, greater religious tolerance and political freedom for intellectual outcasts, offered endless opportunities for those with superior skills and knowledge; it also encouraged the opening of new commercial ventures.

One of these German merchants and international businessmen was Peter Hasenclever from Remscheid, who had become a British subject in 1763 and opened trading ventures in America, Spain, Portugal, France and Britain, dealing in wool, iron and a large number of other commodities with varying success. In 1798 a further increase in trade and boost to the economy was induced by the arrival of wealthier merchants, such as Nathan Mayer Rothschild, the Jewish German banker, businessman, and financier of the Rothschild banking dynasty, who moved from Frankfurt to Manchester in 1798 at the age of twenty-one, bringing his considerable fortune and a network of European connections. He established a business in textile trading and finance before moving to London in 1805 to make a fortune in trading bills-of-exchange through a banking enterprise.[2]

By 1800, German merchant houses had been established in Manchester and Bradford close to the textile mills supplying the world with woven cloth. In 1837 Friedrich Engels Senior, a businessman from the firm of Ermen & Engels in the town of Barmen in the Bergisches Land, founded a spinning factory at Seedley near Pendleton and an office in Manchester. His son, also named Friedrich Engels, who later became an eminent socialist and friend of Karl Marx, was an employee of the firm in Manchester from 1842 to 1850, and from 1864 to 1869 he was even a partner in the firm of Ermen & Engels.[3] In 1871 (the year of Germany's unification) the number of merchants recorded in Britain peaked at 1,084, although it is difficult to estimate exact numbers despite census recordings due to the fact that many merchants were non-permanent residents in Britain. They still entered the country and often remained for longer periods of time, preferring the relaxed way of life in Britain to the more rigorous lifestyle of their homeland.

In comparison with European states and especially Germany, Britain was a liberal and free country and differences of status in society were no longer visible through specific dress codes. Travellers from the continent observed with astonishment that the rich were dressed like the poor and the poor like the rich. They also noted the spirit of freedom among the English population. Many of these travellers came from old established merchant families with widespread national and often international trade connections.[4] Their family networks comprised markets that were new, previously unknown or closed to Britain. They often remained in the country for longer periods to start up new businesses or open the branch of a German company taking advantage of less restrictive trading laws, especially in the production and marketing of textiles.

During the second half of the nineteenth century, and following the boost in trade in textiles and finance, well-educated and well-trained professional groups were attracted by the numerous technological and commercial opportunities revolving around Britain's industrialisation, which can be illustrated by the Great Exhibition of 1851.[5] Although British censuses date from 1801, the first official recordings of immigrants entering Britain on a nationwide scale did not occur until 1861. Besides textiles, Germans also became major suppliers of corn, since Britain had turned from a corn-exporting into a corn-importing country, necessary to feed its rapidly growing population. Imports came from the corn-growing regions of Europe, the Baltic, France and various parts of Germany. German merchants were also involved in the development of trade with Russia, then the import of foreign bar iron and naval stores were 'of strategic importance to the British government, for both military-political and economic reasons'.[6] Also, German merchants involved in the Anglo-Russian trade possessed knowledge of language and culture that the British merchants did not initially have.[7] Cooperation between British, German and Russian merchants contributed towards further relations in new markets, commercial services and know-how and eventually to a closer economic integration of the Tsarist Empire with Europe.

By the beginning of the nineteenth century, Britain had grown into a nation of new (business) ventures with endless opportunities for those who entered the country bringing capital for further investment. Not only were these businessmen carriers of news from distant places, they carried out their business while travelling through Britain on their way to North America and often stayed in the country for only short periods of time. Many of them were German Jews, familiar with newly developing foreign markets and the latest production techniques. They would also send family members to open new branches of their firms, gain experience, and learn the language as apprentices or trainees with foreign partners in Britain's rapidly expanding industrial cities. Not only was there a transfer of capital, but also a transfer of even more trade networks, which spread to other areas of manufacturing such as farming and food processing. This was followed in the later nineteenth century with the large-scale development of metallurgical, chemical, and electrical industries.

Although the second half of the nineteenth century showed a reduction in the numbers of German merchants operating in British markets – with the exception of those who remained in the country to serve international markets – many German merchants and businessmen connected with the textile industry had already migrated to Britain. The wool merchants originally from the north-eastern areas of Germany settled in areas of Britain and then moved to Bradford, which soon became the wool centre of the world. These worldly businessmen built impressive Gothic-style warehouses, which can still be admired in the historical area of Bradford named 'Little Germany'.[8] Cloth merchants settled in Manchester, Liverpool and other textile manufacturing areas. This encouraged the transfer of financial institutions and the engagement of English-speaking agents.

The language problem, known to have been a severe hindrance to business transactions during the Industrial Revolution, encouraged German company owners to send their sons to England for one or two years to work as apprentices, learn the language, and trading practises, not only relating to Great Britain, but also to the British colonies. On the other hand, language problems were becoming apparent in British companies, who often preferred to employ German bilingual clerks in their offices. Germans were said to be well trained and efficient in comparison to their British colleagues, who generally spoke no foreign languages at all. Apart from superior language skills they had also been thoroughly trained – more than their English counterparts – having already served lengthy apprenticeships and attended commercial colleges. A London Chamber of Commerce survey found that 'ninety-nine per cent of the Englishmen who take to commercial life are alleged to have no serviceable acquaintance with French or German'. The result of this dilemma was that employers dealing in foreign trade were compelled to employ foreigners as foreign correspondence clerks. These occupied almost 50 per cent of positions because of the lack of language teaching in Britain.

Low pay, for which German employers were notorious, would have had little effect on these middle and upper class offspring, who often preferred to remain in the country and open new branches of a family business because of the amount of commerce attracted from abroad. This induced a further transfer of capital which came from a variety of sources.

With the development of communications and transport, new modes of long-distance travel by steamship and railroad opened even more opportunities for trade.

Successful Ventures

Not only were the sons of successful merchants eager to open company branches, many poorer migrants were also successful in their search for a better life, despite their origins. The fact that Britain was a free and easy country in comparison to the rigid structures of their homelands made it possible for them, along with the necessary determination, to develop whatever talents they possessed whether it be in the arts, sciences or commerce.

One of the best-known examples is Sir William Herschel (1738–1822). He was an oboist in the German Military Band like his father and also played the violin, harpsichord and organ. At the age of nineteen his father sent him to seek refuge in England following the French invasion of Hanover in 1757. Herschel became a music teacher; he was also the composer of twenty-four symphonies and gave many concertos. In 1766, he became resident organist of the Octagon Chapel in Bath and was appointed Director of Public Concerts.

A meeting with the Royal Astronomer Nevil Maskelyne awoke his interest in mathematics and optics. He began building his own telescopes and, along with the study of distant celestial bodies, he began a systematic search for binary stars. Herschel conducted two preliminary telescopic surveys of the heavens. In 1781, during his third survey of the night sky, he discovered an extraordinary object that was actually the planet Uranus and its two moons, Titania and Oberon. In 1781 Herschel was elected a Fellow of the Royal Society and awarded their Copley Medal. He became famous overnight and as a result of this discovery George III appointed him Court Astronomer.

Herschel later studied the nature of nebulae and discovered that all nebulae were a formation of stars, hence rejecting the long-held belief that nebulae were composed of a luminous fluid. He also discovered two moons of Saturn, Mimas and Enceladus, and coined the term 'asteroid'. Herschel maintained that the solar system is moving through space and found out the direction of that movement. He also suggested that the Milky Way was in the shape of a disk. William Herschel was appointed a foreign member of the Royal Swedish Academy of Sciences in 1813, and was knighted three years later in 1816.[9] He died on 25 August 1822 in Slough, Berkshire at the age of eighty-three. His work was continued by his son, John Herschel.

Another poor trooper who became a wealthy entrepreneur was Ambrose Godfrey Hanckwitz (1660–1741), born in Nienburg in Saxony, who travelled with his wife to London at the age of nineteen. Besides inventing the very first fire extinguisher, he established one of the earliest firms of industrial chemists after inventing a method of producing phosphorus from human urine or faeces using very high temperatures. He was one of the first phosphorus manufacturers, as well as being one of the best and most successful of his time, well known for producing the best phosphorus available, which he sold within Britain and exported to Europe. By the early eighteenth century, Godfrey was thought to be selling as much as 50 lbs a year and making a healthy profit at 50 shillings wholesale or 60 shillings retail an ounce.

In 1707 Godfrey was wealthy enough to buy the lease of a new shop where he opened a pharmacy and he and his family lived above it. Under the terms of the lease he wasn't allowed to carry out his 'obnoxious' trade on the premises, but managed to build a workshop on the narrow strip of land behind the pharmacy instead, where he and his staff made phosphorus and gave demonstrations of its production (it was claimed that he often burnt holes in his trousers). Godfrey died on 15 January 1741. His sons, Ambrose and John, were unsuccessful in the business, which later passed to Ambrose Godfrey, named after his grandfather. The younger Ambrose carried on the business until his death in 1797 and his son, Ambrose Towers Godfrey, formed a partnership with Charles Cooke; the firm Godfrey & Cooke continuing on until 1915.[10]

Members of one of Britain's most wealthy families are the descendants of Johann Baring (1697–1748), who originated from Bremen and was the son of a Lutheran pastor. He came to England as an immigrant at the age of twenty, was apprenticed to a wool merchant and settled at Larkbear near Exeter as a cloth manufacturer.[11] He decided to stay in England, obtained citizenship, and anglicised his name to John.

John, who had proved himself a good trader, married the daughter of a prosperous Exeter businessman. They had four sons and one daughter. When John Baring died in 1748, he was one of the richest merchants in the West Country, and it has been claimed that he was one of only three men in Exeter who kept a carriage – the others being the bishop and the recorder. His descendants include Diana, Princess of Wales, and Prince William, Duke of Cambridge.

JOHN BARING
of Larkbeare.
b. 1697. d. 1748.

John Baring. (Image reproduced courtesy of The Baring Archive).

In 1762, three of his sons – John, Francis, and Charles Baring – established the London merchant house of John & Francis Baring & Co., later known as Baring Brothers. Francis Baring took the lead in managing the business. As a merchant house they carried on with the family tradition, buying and selling goods in Britain and from other countries. They would often work together with other merchants on joint-account and built up a network of contacts. Francis soon realised that there was more to a merchant's life than serge cloth and linen and began trading in more exotic commodities like cochineal, copper and diamonds. He had an original mind and was one of the first bankers to appreciate that the financing of trade agreements could be a more reliable way of making money than trading itself. He began to act on behalf of other merchants; if merchants were based overseas and couldn't be in London to deal with people face to face, he would arrange shipping and insurance, and make and collect payments on their behalf. The business became a merchant bank when Francis Baring began to lend money to these merchants and arrange payments for them.

Once they had entered the world of finance, the Barings began arranging numerous different types of deals for governments and businesses. They helped the British government to finance its war effort in North America, and the United States to purchase the Louisiana territory from the French. After the Napoleonic wars, Barings provided loans to the French government so that they could make reparation payments to the victorious powers. This led the Duc de Richelieu to make the famous statement – 'There are six great powers in Europe, England, France, Prussia, Austria, Russia and the Baring Brothers'. Barings went on to become the London agents representing the governments of Argentina, the United States, Canada and Russia. They also financed projects such as the Canadian Pacific Railway.

During the Industrial Revolution and until the First World War, Barings continued to invest in a great number of international industrial projects. During the Second World War the bank was used by the government to liquidate assets in the USA and around the world in order to provide funds for the war effort.

In 1969 The Baring Foundation was established with the purpose of giving money to charities, with a particular emphasis on social welfare. Of the eight members of the board of the new foundation, five were members of the Baring family. But with the abandonment of currency exchange controls in the early 1980s, Baring was able to focus once again on overseas issues, and was active in bond issues for Finland, Sweden and other countries. Within the United Kingdom the bank played an increasingly significant part in corporate finance, particularly in mergers and acquisitions. It was also increasingly active in investment management for private clients and organizations.

In 1995 a Barings employee, Nick Leeson, lost £827 million due to unauthorised and speculative investing, primarily in futures contracts, at the bank's Singapore office. This was twice the bank's available trading capital.

Barings, founded in 1717 by a young German immigrant, had developed from a small merchant house in Exeter to the second largest bank in the world. It was declared insolvent on 26 February 1995.[12]

During the second half of the nineteenth century, the influx of a sizeable German merchant-class brought further wealth to British industrial cities such as Bradford, Liverpool, Manchester and Glasgow. By the 1860s there were at least sixty-five German firms trading in Bradford. German families who settled in the area played an important role in the cultural and financial development of the city which, again, encouraged the coming of young and ambitious migrants, eager for a chance to climb the social ladder.

One such young man, Robert Johannes Kretzschmar (1866–1952), born in Leipzig, became one of Bradford's most outstanding wool merchants. He enrolled as an apprentice salesman at the Leipzig Kammgarnspinnerei and learnt all the processes of the wool trade from buying to combing, spinning, weaving and selling. At the age of twenty-two he travelled to Bradford. Greatly impressed with the 'Wool City of the World', he decided to settle there and found work as a clerk. He became a naturalised British citizen in 1896 and during the First World War anglicised his surname to Inman.

Robert Inman was co-founder and principal of Inman, Spencer & Co., which soon gained an international reputation as one of the leading businesses in the wool trade. Four of his nine sons represented the business worldwide and two set up on their own as Inman Brothers.

Robert Inman, who spoke French, Greek, Italian, Swedish, German and Latin fluently, also travelled extensively as President of the Bradford Export Merchants Association. He was Vice President of the Bradford Chamber of Commerce and one of the leading figures in the International Wool Textile Organisation.[13]

Skilled Workers

Over the sixteenth and seventeenth centuries, German mining and metallurgical specialists came to Britain, probably at the request of the English court. In 1528, the Augsburg merchant Joachim Höchstetter was named 'Principal Surveyor of all Mines in England and Ireland'. He obtained the right to search for gold, silver, copper and lead in England, Wales and Ireland. In July 1564, a group of Tyrolese miners arrived at Keswick to begin work.

Another partnership was formed between the German Christoph Schütz and the Englishman William Humfrey to exploit copper and silver ore for the manufacture of cannons, household ware from copper, and the production of iron wire. Schütz also introduced into England the drawing of iron wire and the use of the straining hammer. By the beginning of the seventeenth century, activities had declined because the yield had been lower than expected.

However, a number of German specialists in metallurgical trades settled in the mining districts of Westmorland, Cumberland and Wales to introduce the manufacture of brass wire, copper plating and other brass articles. English apprentices learned the manufacture of brassware from these German skilled workers and the production of English brass increasingly rivalled that of other well-known continental centres.

Similarly, the manufacture of sewing needles was introduced to England by German craftsmen, invited by Queen Elizabeth during the mid-sixteenth century. Consequently, English needle making rivalled the German industry and gained superiority by developing the process of making needles by machines.

In the latter part of the seventeenth century, a group of swordsmiths and cutlers from Solingen in Germany, known as the 'City of Blades', since it has long been renowned for the manufacturing of fine swords, knives, scissors, razors and cutlery, broke their guild oaths by taking their production secrets with them and settling in Shotley Bridge, County Durham. Later they moved to Birmingham and were also successful in boosting the steel industry in Sheffield. Johann Jacob Holzapfel, who was renowned for his skill in making thread-cutting tools and tools for lathes, settled in London. The mechanic Andreas Friedrich Bauer was joined in 1806 by Friedrich Koenig, the inventor of the mechanical printing press and by 1814 *The Times* was printed on such a press. In 1800 Matthias Koops established a factory for the manufacture of paper from materials other than linen and cotton rags at Millbank near Westminster Bridge. Many of these businessmen received financial support from either the Crown or other wealthy persons. Others attracted the attention of merchants, manufacturers or guilds, which often caused opposition from English competitors.[14]

Settling in a new country meant learning the language and climbing the social ladder. Letters were written home advertising for workers, offering board and lodging, which also reduced household expenses. Attracted by descriptions of successful business ventures and offers of jobs to friends and relatives, chain-migration followed by those who preferred the comparatively short journey to Britain rather than undertaking the long and hazardous voyage to the other side of the world. These lower class migrants were absent in modern industrial sectors such as textiles and engineering, but were employed in traditional trades, such as butchers, bakers, tailors, shoemakers, clockmakers and office clerks.

The Sugar Bakers

This was the term used to describe workers in the sugar houses or refineries that were abundant in the East End of London. The areas around Whitechapel were close to the Port of London, where huge quantities of raw sugar arrived from the West Indian colonies.

With the growing popularity of coffee and tea in the eighteenth century came the demand for refined or 'improved' sugar, which had previously been sold in brown loafs weighing up to 7 lbs. In 1753 there were eighty sugar refiners (entrepreneurs) in London. Each of them employed an average of fifteen German workers who dominated the trade as a result of chain migration. A large number of sugar bakers had learnt the trade in Hanover, North Germany, which at that time was the centre of the sugar-refining industry. By 1800 the annual consumption of sugar had grown to 20 lbs per head. The workforce of some bigger refineries numbered up to a hundred workers who were willing to transfer their knowledge to unskilled workers. So doing, they played a vital role in the development of British sugar refining, which was wholly dependent upon skilled workers, described in the 'Statistical Society's Report of 1848' as 'cleanly, orderly, and well conducted body of men, chiefly worshippers at the German chapel in the neighbourhood'. It has been said that even the British Consul in Germany acted as an agent for companies who preferred to import their own labour.

Through constant boiling the raw sugar was turned it into powder, which was again diluted before entering the oven to be 'baked into a loaf'. Before technical improvements in the mid-nineteenth century, this was a dangerous trade with risks of fire and explosion; workers were exposed to boiling sugar, scorching containers, scalding steam, heavy objects, poor building design, and fire. There were no precautions regarding 'Health and Safety'. Workers risked their lives doing hot, exhausting and dangerous work and instead of continuing in their father's footsteps many second-generation Germans often preferred less dangerous work, which brought about further recruitment from Germany. In the census of 1861 it was recorded that 1,345 Germans were occupied as sugar refiners in England and Wales, which also included sugar brokers. In the mid-nineteenth century sugar workers formed the second strongest occupational group among all German immigrants, even though some happened to be registered as 'labourers'. This leads to the assumption that their numbers might have been larger.[15]

James Greenwood describes his visit to a sugar-baking factory in his essay 'The Wilds of London', published in 1876 by Chatto & Windus:

> At a sugar baking:
> I cannot give the name of the bakery selected, as I have clean forgotten it; but the reader will be at no loss on that score, since I was given to understand that one system regulates the business and that one bakery is as much like another as peas of a pod. It is by no means a hole-and-corner business, as one might be led to imagine

it was, judging from the rare occasions of its being brought under public notice. In the neighbourhood of Back-church-Lane, in Whitechapel, there are dozens of these baking, or, as they would more properly be called, boiling-houses. They are buildings enormous in size, usually occupying the whole of a street side, and so high that the massy 'mats' of sugar craned up to the topmost story, and there dangling from its chains, looks no bigger or more substantial than a fishmonger's rush-basket that the wind might blow away.

A kind-hearted German missionary was my companion, and soon as I put my head in at the door of the bakery, the nature of the manufacture in progress was at once made apparent to my senses. Just as unmeasured indulgence in sugar is nauseating to the palate, so was the reek of it palling to one's sense of smell. You could taste its clammy sweetness on the lips just as the salt of the sea may be so discovered while the ocean is yet a mile away.

It was a sort of handy outer warehouse, that to which we were first introduced – a low-roofed, dismal place with grated windows, and here and there a foggy little gas-jet burning blear-eyed against the wall. The walls were black – not painted black. As far as one might judge they were bare brick, but 'basted' unceasingly by the luscious steam that enveloped the place, they had become coated with a thick preserve of sugar and grime. The floor was black, and all corrugated and hard, like a public thoroughfare after a shower and then a frost. The roof was black and pendent from the great supporting posts and balks of timber were sooty, glistening icicles and exudings like those of the gum-tree. ...At the extremity of this gloomy cave, and glowing duskily at the mouth of a narrow passage, was dimly visible a gigantic globular structure in bright copper, and hovering about it a creature with bare arms and chest all grizzly-haired, with a long bright rod of iron in his grasp, which incessantly he waved about the mighty caldron; this was doubtless the Sugar Ogre himself, in waiting for juvenile delinquents. Being in no dread of the ogre, however, we approached him, and discovered him to be a very civil fellow, quietly minding his business. The copper structure above-mentioned proved to be nothing more necromantic than a gigantic pan, in which were, gently seething, ten tons of liquid sugar. The vessel was all covered in, and looked as compact as an orange, the shape of which fruit it resembles; but in the side of it there was a small disc of glass, and looking through it one could get a glimpse of the bubbling straw-coloured mass within. The iron rod the guardian of the pan called a 'key,' if I rightly remember, and his sole occupation appeared to consist in dipping it in at a little hole in the vessel's side, and withdrawing it again, along with a little blob of melted sugar, which he took between his finger and thumb, and drew out and examined by the light of the gas.

From this we were conducted to the factory where the manufacturers of moist sugar were working. ... Some sugars are prepared at the place of their growth, and sent here ready for immediate use; but the great bulk of it is exported in a very rough state, dense, strong smelling, and of the colour of mahogany, and before it can be brought to assume the bright and inviting appearance it bears when ticketed in the grocer's window it has to undergo much torture by fire and machinery.

It was not a nice-looking place that to which we were introduced. It was not a pleasant way that led to it, inasmuch as it was in an underground direction and through passages gloomy, low-roofed, and narrow, and lit with gas just enough to show all manner of wriggling and revolving machinery overhead and threading the walls. Down we went, however – our conductor kindly making the passage safer by illumining it by means of an old newspaper hastily twisted into a torch, and there we were in full view of the makers of moist sugar.

The place was nothing but a vast cellar underground, and lit from without only by a window here and there high up where the street pavement was, and as closely grated as though it were an object to keep flies out of the factory.

The heat was sickening and oppressive, and an unctuous steam, thick and foggy, filled the cellar from end to end... Seeming, as it were, to grow out of the dense haze, busy figures appeared. ... On one side of the cellar were two gigantic pans of sugar, melted and hot and smoking, and out of these the labourers, naked but for a covering for their legs and some sort of apron, and their bodies bathed in sweat, and their fair hair reeking and hanging lank about their wan faces, scooped up the liquor into the pails, that would contain half a hundred weight, and hurried across the cellar to deposit it in vast revolving basins set in motion at lightning speed by machinery, and where the brown sugar was bleached and dried, to be presently shovelled out and added to the great heap that reached high nearly as the ceiling. ... 'They'd be dead without their beer unlimited,' remarked our guide. 'And does it not hurt them?' 'Well, it helps to knock them off, I dare say, so that it amounts to the same thing, only that the unlimited beer-drinker of the sugar bakery has the advantage of lengthy dying.'

Out of this cellar and through others similarly occupied, and then upstairs, and here to be sure was another strange sight. This was a branch of the loaf-sugar department. It was an extensive floor, a hundred feet by seventy probably, and covering the whole of it were packed loaf-sugar moulds as closely as the cells of a beehive are arranged. The moulds were stuck point downwards into earthen jars that at once upheld them and served as receptacles for their 'drainings'. I do not understand the process that was then operating, but what was to be seen was a dozen men of the semi-naked sort like those below crawling like frogs over the surface of the sugar moulds, getting foot and hand hold on the edges, some with a sort of engine hose squirting a transparent liquor into the moulds, and others stirring the thick stuff constantly in the latter with their hands.

Upstairs again; up crystallized stairs with 'toffee' for a handrail and hardbake to knock your head against if you were not aware of impending beams, to a room likewise full of moulds (they turn out twelve thousand loaves a week at this establishment), but where the greatest novelty to the eye of the uninitiated are many heaps of what in appearance is the exact counterpart of mud off the public roads. It was not so, however, as the guide explained it; it was merely the scrapings of beams and the shovelling of floors and gangways, and workshops, and it was intended for filtration through charcoal after which it would be deemed worthy to take its place as a marketable commodity.

Upstairs again – the place seemed to grow hotter the higher we climbed; and here was the 'filling' department, the place where the moulds were filled with liquid sugar that flowed out of great taps. This, it seemed, was the hardest part of the sugar-baking business. Like every hand in the establishment, with the exception of the foreman and over-lookers, the labourers here were midway nude (the disgusting practice is evidently one of habit rather than necessity among German sugar-bakers; we saw in one room – a comparatively cool room – half a dozen fellows squatted down engaged in the not over-heating occupation of painting moulds, but they were as naked as the rest). The moulds, as we were informed when filled with the melted sugar, weigh a hundred-weight and a half, and the liquid, as it runs, is hot. The task to be performed is to fill the moulds at the taps and carry them across the great warehouses and arrange them close together for 'setting', each in its own jar in the manner already described. A gang of a dozen or so are so employed, and as the work is piece work, hurry is the order of the day. But hurry is not easy with a hundredweight-and-a-half of sloppy hot sugar to carry in an inconvenient vessel, and the result is that as they shuffle off in line with their loads there are many lurches, and stumblings, and elbowings, and the contents of the moulds hugged to the chest slop over the naked bodies of the carriers, and then harden and crust to a coat, doubtless as inconvenient to wear as it is disgusting to behold.

No wonder that the poor wretches so employed drink much beer. With no more exertion than leisurely walking about demanded, before I had been in the factory a quarter of an hour, I was drenched with perspiration, and was not a moment free from a trickling down my face. To be sure, since indulgence in beer assists the sugar-baker in his work it is commendable in the master to provide it. But, as I am informed, it is in his power to carry his kindness a step further – he can abridge the sugar-baker's labouring hours. The poor fellow's wages are quite as low as those of the Irish hodman, but, unlike the last-mentioned, he knows nothing of a 'nine-hours-law'. The sugar-baker works all hours. What he calls a fair day's work is twelve hours, but it is not rare for him to be kept at the slavery above described for sixteen, and even eighteen hours – from three o'clock in the morning till eight at night – without a penny of overtime or extra pay. He cannot help himself. If he leaves one factory he must enter another exactly similar. It is a sight, I am told, to meet a group of the poor fellows just hurried from their beds, and making haste to their work at three o'clock of a winter's morning. Unrested, shivering, pale, and aguish, they are eager to get back to the heat and the beer; they need 'warming

Sugar-making at the Counterslip Refinery, Bristol; W. B. Murray, *The Illustrated London News*, 29 November 1873. (© Alamy Limited).

up' as they say, and that object effected, they manage to potter through the weary day somehow and then they shuffle home to bed, and so on between Sunday and Saturday. The only time, my good missionary friend informed me – and he should know – when you can catch sight of a sugar-baker neither abed nor at work is on a Sunday afternoon when he enjoys the luxury of idleness and a pipe at his own door or window.

Until the mid-nineteenth century, the sugar industry was concentrated in London's East End, in Whitechapel, St. George's-in-the-East, and Mile End New Town. From the 1860s onwards traditional sugar refining began to decline dramatically, giving way to larger and modern refineries that employed several hundred working men. These were established by successful Scottish (Abram Lyle) and north English (Henry Tate) entrepreneurs in an area bordering on East London, whereby 20 per cent of the 500-man workforce still consisted of Hanoverian sugar bakers. When the industry began to spread to other parts of Britain, this indicated the overall decline of German business interests. By 1911, the sugar bakers were almost non-existent.[16]

The Food and Hospitality Industry

Traditional cooking plays an important role in ethnic identity. When Germans began entering the country during the late Middle Ages, they also imported their food habits.

By the mid-nineteenth century, the size of the German community in the east and west ends of London supported enough shops selling German products and traditional foods to encourage more people to settle in the area and open more businesses. Although there were German communities in major northern cities such as Liverpool, Manchester, Bradford and Glasgow, these remained small in size compared to London – the east and west ends being the heartland of the German community in Britain. By 1913 the main thoroughfare of the West End – Charlotte Street – counted at least forty German names out of the 138 businesses listed. These included delicatessen food shops, German pork butchers, a mustard factory, which produced and sold different types of German mustards, and bakeries selling exquisite pastries and cakes, as well as wine shops.[17] An article in *The Times* of 28 February 1910 claimed that 'The German baker flaunts his name over the palatial shops in the West End and is equally evident in the slums of the East End'. Not only did they produce different types of Rye and 'Black Bread', they also worked as confectioners and attracted their customers with delicate cakes and tortes.

One of the best-known German bakeries in Britain was the Matthes Bakery, founded by the brothers Wilhelm and Ludwig Matthes, who originated from the village of Braunsbach where their family had established a guest house and bakery. Wilhelm and his young brother left Germany and headed for England to seek fame and fortune. Their skills as Matthes bakers enabled the opening of a small bakery in Rotherhithe in London. From there, Wilhelm Ludwig's son, Louis, moved to East Anglia. In 1898, the first Matthes bakery opened in England's Lane, Gorleston-on-Sea. Over the next eighty years, the family baking business thrived with thirty-three outlets bearing the Matthes name and traded for many years as 'The Sunshine Bread' bakery, with satellite bakeries and shops covering much of East Anglia. A restaurant was later opened in England's Lane and in Yarmouth town centre. Sadly, they were bought out by the Spiller Flour Company, which itself folded in 1978. A 200-year-old tradition of baking bread was broken with the closure of the Matthes bakeries in that year.[18]

Restaurants and hotels began to emerge at the beginning of the nineteenth century; a trade previously unknown in Britain. The concept of eating out in a restaurant had originated in Paris and gradually spread throughout Europe. This new form of 'entertainment' gradually spread throughout Great Britain during the Victorian era until the First World War. To transform eating into an entertainment experience, where one was relieved of the chores of preparing a meal and be waited upon instead, allowed diners to meet friends, converse freely and enjoy the food. This new experience was served by both a native and foreign labour force from continental European countries such as France, Switzerland and Austria-Hungary, although German-speaking waiters were the largest in numbers.

Therefore, migrants have played a central role in the evolution of the eating-out patterns in Britain. They have also introduced a transfer of skills, expertise and knowledge of products that have, until the present day, influenced the domestic eating (and drinking) habits of the population as a whole.[19]

In 1861, German waiters and servants in Britain (mostly in London) numbered 380. Over the following five decades numbers increased and the census of 1911 recorded 4,721 servants and waiters.[20] Although waiting occupations were poorly paid and workers remained poor, ethnic solidarity existed in nineteenth century Britain among the German community and new arrivals would be assisted in finding work and accommodation. Trade organisations connected with occupational groups, employment agencies and journals such as the *London Hotel and Restaurant Employees Gazette* helped migrants to become accustomed to their new country. The history of restaurants in Britain, therefore, is closely connected with the arrival of Germans with a strong desire to learn English. German and Swiss hoteliers sent their sons to Britain to gain trade experience and learn English. With the increase of British and American travellers to Europe, a strong demand had developed for English-speaking staff in the hospitality industry. Having gained the necessary experience, many preferred to remain in Britain, having grown as accustomed to the easy-going lifestyle as to that of their homeland.

Dining out in a Victorian restaurant around 1850. (© Alamy Limited).

Eventually, they would open their own hotel or restaurant selling German food and Lager beer to meet the growing demand of both British and German consumers.[21]

The long-established Tennents Brewery in Glasgow started to add Lager beer to its range of products in the early 1890s and for this purpose brought in German brewers, chemists and engineers for this flourishing market which was the main attraction in many restaurant and beer hall advertisements. An advertisement by Löwenbräu in the *Londoner General Anzeiger* of 3 January 1900 listed seventeen establishments in London that sold this beer, proving the growing popularity of traditional German beer-drinking culture:

> Underneath the London Pavilion music hall was a beer cellar which announced its presence by a large shining red spade trade mark — Spatenbrau. There you could get the best glass of lager in London, there you could get the 'dunkel Lager' — the 'München-Löwenbräu' — just as one drank it in Germany. There is a good bar there still. But it is no longer the Spaten.
>
> Across the road, at the top of the Haymarket, was another landmark. Here you could get a light meal and a drink free from any annoyance or the importunity of the prostitutes who thronged the Circus. Appenrodt's was a famous delicatessen shop; it was cheap and superlatively good. There were Continental delicacies of all kinds; sausages in bewildering variety, wonderful Salami, splendid Lager and coffee it was a privilege to drink. When the First World War came an English firm took over and of course it was never the same.[22]

The Royal Mail was a German restaurant and beer hall, located near the City (two minutes from the main post office). It was open from 7.00 a.m. until 11.30 p.m., offering a good selection of German and English food. The following examples taken from a selection of advertisements from 1901 are a reminder of when Germans were a significant minority in London. They offer comfortable surroundings for customers to drink, shop, read, eat, learn and socialise with their fellow countrymen and women.

'Im Deutschen Haus' (The 'German House'), run by L. Treibel, offered the German guest the best food and service in London: lunch on weekdays was 8*d,* Sundays and holidays 9*d*; rooms at 3*s* – 3*s*, 6*d* per week, or 8*d* – 9*d* per night; warm and cold meals at all hours of the day; money exchange services; tobacco, cigars, cigarettes; free information and work permits for barbers and hairdressers. Tickets sold for passages to Hamburg, Bremen, Africa and America German newspapers were also available.

The expansion of the middle classes in Britain during the nineteenth century and the increase in the number of restaurants in London led to the introduction of the French cuisine in Britain. Migrants established two of the most famous dining houses in Britain before 1914; the Café Royal in Regent Street, which was opened by Daniel de Nicols, a French wine merchant, and Cesar Ritz, the thirteenth son of a Swiss shepherd who worked his way through the continent and founded the hotel in 1906, which bears his name. Similarly, they imported continental staff. The famous French chef, August Escoffier, became known as the first modern celebrity chef when he came to England to revolutionise the art of cooking.[23] In the census of 1861, only 251 foreign cooks were recorded in England and Wales. In 1900 the Society of German Chefs was founded and recorded a membership of about 100. This also served as an employment agency for a number of years. By 1901 the number of foreign cooks employed in Great Britain had increased to 2,447 persons, making this one of the most important occupations for foreigners.

A historical postcard of 'Appenrodt's delicatessen shop.'

Deutsches Restaurant und Lagerbierhalle
„ROYAL MAIL,"
17, Noble Street, Falcon Square, E.C.
(Zwei Minuten vom Hauptpostamt).

Gute deutsche und englische Küche.

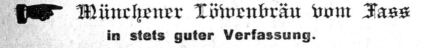

☞ **Münchener Löwenbräu vom Fass**
in stets guter Verfassung.

Geöffnet von morgens **7** Uhr bis abends **11½** Uhr.

H. ANDRESS, Eigentümer
(früher Besitzer des „RODENSTEIN," Islington)

— I —

The Royal Mail was a German restaurant and beer hall. (© Bishopsgate Institute, London – Special Collections and Archives).

Im Deutschen Haus. (© Bishopsgate Institute, London – Special Collections and Archives).

The most important occupation in the catering trade among Germans in Britain before 1914, however, was that of the waiter. Referring to the 1901 census, it can be estimated that a total of 8,634 foreign waiters were working throughout the country, of whom 3,039 were Germans.[24] German waiters were organised in various trade organisations. The Deutsche Kellnerverein (German Waiters Club), which was founded as early as 1869, had approximately 600 members by the turn of the century and their annual ball was attended by hundreds of people. Members wore a black, red and gold cockade adorned with a small silver corkscrew. It was attached to the largest body, 'The Ganymede Friendly Society for Hotel and Restaurant Employees', which had 2,000 members and twenty-five local branches throughout Britain by 1913 – charmingly named 'Union Ganymede'. It aimed to support new arrivals in their search for work as well as to provide a platform for conviviality. The substantial clubhouse in London had 'rooms for offices and committees, a dining-hall, a concert hall holding three-hundred people, a billiard room with six tables, a skittle-alley, sports-hall, library and fifty-five bedrooms. There were also clubhouses in Manchester and Liverpool'.[25]

Other Edwardian organisations concentrated on different trade aspects, such as 'The Caterers Employees Union', which represented the branch of a larger organisation based in Hamburg. This particular group attended to the working conditions of all those involved in the catering trade as well as the London-based 'Christian Association for Hospitality Support Staff', which was the centre of a worldwide network of activity.

These variable types of trade organisations prevented German waiters from entering a vacuum on their arrival in Britain. They moved into, and within, pre-existing occupational and social networks, which eased the 'migration shock' and helped them to establish themselves in the British labour market.

German Pork Butchers

They contributed largely towards the production of tasty meals and affordable cuts of meat for working class customers and were highly popular among factory workers. Very little was previously known about these migrants, originally butchers from a region in south Germany called Hohenlohe in the north-eastern region of the Kingdom of Württemberg, a Germanic state once located within what is now the federal state of Baden-Württemberg. The historian Karl-Heinz Wüstner uncovered this piece of unknown history in 1993 while researching the history of craftsmanship in church archives in his native Hohenlohe.

Between 1806 and 1952, Baden-Württemberg was one of numerous German-speaking independent kingdoms in the southwest regions of Germany. Economic migration took off in the mid-nineteenth century after agricultural land had been divided into a multitude of tiny holdings after the abolition of serfdom, resulting in farmers often being unable to support their families.[26] Also, the inheritance system gave land to the eldest or most qualified son, which made it necessary for other male siblings to seek a living elsewhere. In many cases, the only way to maintain social and economic status was migration. In the archives, a significant number of male migrants were described as pork-butchers, although it can be concluded that these would have been predominantly pig-breeders and small-holder farmers. Having attended butchery courses during the winter months when farm work slowed down[27], they were familiar with traditional methods of cooking and preserving pork. Many households had their own traditional recipes for salting, pickling and smoking meat, passed down from generation to generation. The poorer cuts and the scraps were finely minced and with a sufficient amount of pork fat, herbs, seasonings and spices, as well as occasionally potato starch, were turned (often smoked) into that most economical of meat products, the sausage, of which there was and still is a huge variety in Germany.

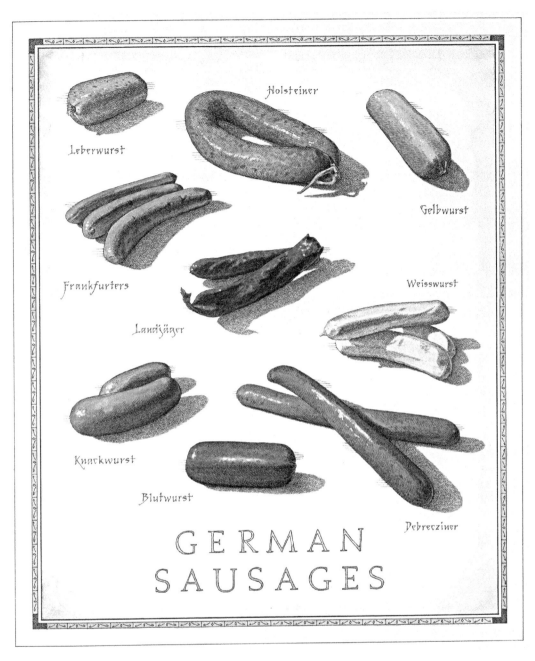

German Sausages. (© John Burgoyne illustration).

As in many agricultural areas of Germany during the nineteenth century, crop failure, population growth, hunger and poverty had been the cause of mainstream emigration across the Atlantic Ocean to North America. However, a large number of young men and women from the small town of Kunzelsau in Baden Württemberg, all within a radius of 20 miles of each other, chose England as their new homeland. Britain was close; transport was easy and relatively cheap (steamboats began sailing the Rhine in the 1840s) compared with the price of a ships passage to the other side of the world.

Besides the strong links which had existed for centuries between the two countries, Britain had become the fastest growing industrial nation of that time, with plenty of opportunities for the young, strong and ambitious. Migrants were eager to practice their skills and trades in this rapidly expanding economy, and willing to work hard for higher social esteem and a better standard of living than could be achieved in their homeland. Also, in pre-refrigeration days, these German immigrants were familiar with different methods of preserving meat. Accordingly, they discovered a population with a great appetite for meat that most workers were unable to afford. The German sausage used very little of this expensive product and stretched it even further. Sausages soon became immensely popular among British factory workers, cooked on an open fire instead of the oven, which many households were lacking. For workers sharing rooms in multiple-occupancy houses with little comfort, this was the only way they could cook.

Using their singular knowledge and skills eager to avoid competition with British butchers, who dealt mostly in beef and mutton or lamb, stories of success soon triggered chain migration. Letters were written home with requests for manpower – youngsters eager to learn a trade and young women for work or even for marriage. Church records show that a large percentage of Germans chose marriage partners of the same nationality, although marriages did take place between German men and British women. However, in the case of the pork butchers and other ethnic or family-run businesses, requests would be sent home for suitable partners and so it can be reasonably assumed that frequent chain migration existed in these family businesses and many single German women from Hohenlohe entered the country with the prospect finding work and perhaps also marriage.

Records show that the first professional pork butcher to settle in England was Johann Michael Ebert, who opened his shop in Sheffield in 1817, followed by Christian Friedrich Ebert, who in 1825 also settled in Sheffield. Soon a steady flow of German butchers from Hohenlohe began entering the country. They were followed by the sons of farmers, small-holders and tradesmen; not professional butchers, but eager to learn the trade from friends and relatives already in Britain who needed manpower, often in exchange for board and lodging and a small allowance. Having then learnt the trade, they would move to another of the many industrial cities of Great Britain and also set up in business. This was made possible by the structural changes in Britain during the industrial revolution with rapidly growing towns and cities. A more liberal and open-minded society compared to that of their homeland made integration less difficult and one can clearly state that they were admired for their German virtues of discipline and hard work. Although they were closely tied, often by marriage and within small communities, they kept to their traditions as an element of distinction on the one hand, and on the other hand they were able to assimilate into the communities they served.

In Sheffield, the number of German pork butcher shops had risen to fourteen by 1883.[28] In the census of 1861, 244 German butchers were recorded in England and Wales, which by 1881 had grown to 730 and peaked at 1,224 shops in 1901[29], mostly situated in the northern industrial cities where there was an urgent need for cheap and tasty meals.

The pork butchers became highly popular among factory workers for keeping their shops open late at night to serve cheap and tasty food to those who worked long hours and had no time to cook. The demand and the market conditions were ripe for what was to become the first 'takeaway' products.[30]

Another name that stands out is Georg Friedrich Ziegler who came to England in 1899 with only a few shillings in his pocket. He prospered well; business grew and they branched out and opened new shops. They gave to charity and helped the poor; gave soup and bread to the hungry and those out of work in the Great Depression of 1926. In 1928 George Frederick Ziegler owned five shops and founded the firm Farm Stores Ltd. In 1965, he was lauded 'as one of Wakefield's most successful businessmen' as senior chairman of Associated Dairies & Farm Stores Ltd – one of the predecessors of today's ASDA supermarket chain.[31]

George Kristian Haffner arrived in England in 1879 at the age of sixteen and went to work for his uncle in Carlisle who already had a well-established pork butcher's business. In 1889, he opened his own pork butcher's shop in Burnley accompanied by his wife, Karoline Rummler, another German immigrant who he married in Carlisle. Burnley was chosen as the location for the business as the anticipated boom in cotton weaving was about to take off, as indeed is what happened.

A major factor of the business was to provide tasty, cheap, and convenient food from a convenient location with the help of their growing family of nine adults who lived over the shop and worked long hours. At the outbreak of the First World War, three of their sons – Bill, Harry and George – joined the Army. George was awarded the Military Medal and Croix de Guerre for bravery in the field.

The enterprise prospered as the industrial population grew with a traditional range of meat products and a range of continental and specifically German sausages. It is interesting to note that the seasoning recipe for their sausages today is still exactly the one brought to England from Germany by Georg Kristian Haffner.[32]

The butchery business from George Haffner & Sons has since flourished for three generations. (© Eileen Haffner, George Haffner (Foods) Ltd, Burnley).

4

GERMAN CULTURE

Musicians

By the beginning of the eighteenth century, when George I, the first of the Hanoverian kings, ascended the British throne in 1714, Germany already had a vigorous musical culture. By the early eighteenth century, music had become immensely popular due to a sound musical education that had spread throughout the country, having been actively encouraged by independent courts and wealthy municipalities.[1] In contrast, there had been no famous British musicians worth mentioning for a number of years. For this reason, and due to a system of patronage that encouraged foreign musicians to come to London, German musicians were welcome in Britain. Therefore, Germany was ripe for the export of musicians who could be classed as trans-migrants; entering Britain with the intention of returning home after periods of seasonal work.

Opportunities for musicians were manifold in London, which became one of Europe's most important centres of music, resulting in the rise of public concerts and the opening of concert halls. Much to the frustration of British musicians, concert promoters sought to attract talented musicians from abroad. George Friedrich Handel was a frequent visitor to the country and later Johann Christian Bach, who became Queen Charlotte's music-master in 1763. Towards the end of the century, Amadeus Mozart and Joseph Haydn also spent periods of time in Britain.[2] Subscription concerts were established, an Italian opera was founded in London, and by the end of the century music had become an integral part of the burgeoning culture of the middle classes.

According to research, a database of some 290 individuals allows for structural insights into the professional group of German musicians in London during this period of time. Some were respected composers or leaders; others performed at the opera, on the stage or as music teachers. They had a considerable influence in the training and development of English musicians who often spent a period of time in London to be taught by German musicians before pursuing their careers elsewhere.[3] These German musicians were also involved in the founding of a charitable friendly society for musicians who had fallen upon hard times for one reason or another. The fund, which was established for the destitute families of insolvent or deceased musicians, was actively supported by George Friedrich Handel, who took part in its annual benefit concert and later bequeathed £1,000 for its use in his will. In 1790 it was granted a Royal Charter and named 'The Royal Society of Musicians'. Its influence continues to this day and still exists for the relief of distress and poverty among professional musicians and their dependants.

Many German musicians were members of marching bands. Military music had become very popular after the Seven Years War (1756–1763) when British regiments would return home with a regimental band of German musicians, who would later become street musicians.[4]

Many belonged to 'village bands', who would return home to Germany and practise throughout the winter months under the supervision of a 'Captain'; these included youths between the ages of twelve and fourteen who were often the victims of exploitation. In the spring they came to Hull and tramped through the country playing at various towns on their way. There were often rich pickings and they would return home at the end of the season with their pockets full of money. Others found their place in theatre orchestras or as music teachers. There are only a few recordings of German musicians having become British nationals – the reason probably being that musicians did not require fixed premises to work.

Henry Mayhew, in his book *Life and Labour of the London Poor*, records an interview with a German musician, who he described as a 'flaxen-haired and fresh coloured young man who spoke English fairly reasonably'.

I have been six years in this country and was 14 years old when I came. I come from Oberfeld, which is 18 miles from Hanover and came here because I heard that London was a good place for foreign music. Another 6 came over with me, boys and men. We came to Hull and played around that area for about half a year and did 'middling'. And then we came to London. I didn't make much money at first because I had a lot to learn, but the band did very well. We were seven. I play the clarinet and so do two others – two play the French horn, one trombone and one saxhorn. Sometimes we each make 7s or 8s a day now but the business is not so good. I reckon that 6s a day is good now. We never play at fairs or for caravans. We play at private parties or public ballrooms and are paid so much a dance – 6 pence a dance for the seven of us. If there are many dances it is good, if not it is bad. We play cheaper than the English and we don't spend so much. The English players insult us but we don't care about that. They abuse us for playing cheap. I don't know what their terms for dances are. I have saved very little money in this country. I want to save enough to take me back to Hanover. We all live together, the seven of us. We have three rooms to sleep in and one room to eat in. We are all single men but one and his wife, a German woman, lives with us and cooks for us. She and her husband have a bedroom to themselves. Anything does for us to eat. We all join in housekeeping and lodging and pay alike. Our lodging costs 2 shillings a week each – our board costs us about 15s. a week each and sometimes less. But that includes beer; the London beer is very good and sometimes we drink a good deal of it. We drink very little gin but live very well and have good meals every day. We play in the streets and I think most places like us. Ladies and gentlemen are our best friends; the working people give us very little. We play opera tunes chiefly and don't associate with any Englishmen. There are three German public houses where we Germans meet, including sugar bakers and other trades. There are now five German brass bands with thirty-seven performers in them including our own, in London. Our band lives near Whitechapel.

Germans were not only excellent musicians and teachers of music, they also thrived as music publishers and makers of musical instruments – working conditions being far better in Britain than on the continent. In 1761 Johann Christoph Zumpe from Nuremberg established a workshop in Hanover Square in London, near the Hanover Square Rooms or the Queen's Concert rooms which was the principal concert venue in London and visited by many leading musicians.[5] Johann Christoph Zumpe made a fortune in the manufacture of pianos, some of which were exported to Germany.

Piano – Johann Christoph Zumpe; Johann Christian Bach advertised having played on a Zumpe-Instrument. Image supplied by Dreweatts and Bloomsbury auctions – early keyboard instruments.

Built between 1760 and 1800, his instruments were smaller and therefore required less room space than a standard piano. They were also less complicated and economical in the production, which made them a popular item with both amateur and professional musicians.

George Miller, who built the first (boxwood) clarinet in England, was said to have originated from Germany.[6] He announced his retirement in the *World* on 19 May 1791 and handed over his business to apprentice John Cramer.

> To the NOBILITY and GENTRY, my PATRONS, in particular, and the PUBLIC in general. I Beg leave most respectfully to inform them, that I have, from my great age and infirmities, thought proper to appoint Mr JOHN CRAMER to carry on my business of a MUSICAL INSTRUMENT-MAKER and TURNER, at No. 3, Dacre-street, Broadway, Westminster, he being a person duly qualified for that purpose, having been taught such business under my particular inspection; and I most humbly solicit for him the future favours of my kind friends and patrons. I beg leave also to assure them, that no other person whatever is authorised by me to carry on the said trade; and to caution them against anyone who hath, or hereafter may, assume my name. It is also necessary for me to observe, that my future support is derived entirely from Mr CRAMER. I have the honour to be, With the greatest deference and respect, Their most obedient humble servant, GEORGE MILLER. No. 3, Dacre-street, Westminster.

There were often close relationships within the community of musicians. Gratitude for the help received during difficult times was regularly recorded in letters and wills. Catherine Bisset gratefully recounts the music lessons given to her as a child after the untimely death of her father, which eventually enabled her to work as a musician and so feed her family – the music teacher she mentioned, a Mr John Cramer, had apparently taught her without charging a fee. John Cramer must surely have been the previously mentioned person, apprenticed to George Miller, the musical instrument-maker who eventually inherited his business.[7]

The general structural features of German musicians in London can be illustrated by the biography of the Griesbach family of musicians who originated from Coppenbrügge near Hanover. As children, they were taught various instruments from a very early age by their father who was the 'town musician'. They also fulfilled various engagements at private and public functions. George Griesbach travelled to England in April 1778 at the age of twenty-one, to become a member of Queen Charlotte's private band, which was also known as 'The Queen's German Band'. George III was a keen lover of music and a good friend to many musicians. The private band played for the king and queen on a daily basis (sometimes several times a day). As soon as a vacancy arose in the band George recommended each of his four younger brothers who played an assortment of instruments, until eventually all five were in London working as court musicians and escorting the king and queen on their travels. Although the Griesbach family were talented musicians, not all of them achieved financial success. George Griesbach was known to be badly in debt. His brother Charles also died penniless, although the queen paid most of his debts. Frederick, a celebrated oboist, fell into debt and died a broken man in 1825. William, a well-known violinist, died in 1825 and left annuities worth £4,000. Second generation Griesbachs were widely known as performers and teachers. One of George's sons, a vicar, was a founder member of the Entomological Society in London.[8]

Teachers and Governesses

In Germany, more and more daughters from educated families were eager to train and work as teachers, this being the only profession open to women that enabled them to maintain their social standing. Also, for daughters of more humble backgrounds, becoming a teacher was a means of social advancement; they were able to learn the job by 'learning by doing', or from 1840 onwards enrol in one of the numerous public and private training institutions for teachers and governesses, which ended with a formal examination. They could often be classed as 'trans-migrants' and in many cases entered Britain with the intention of returning home, especially in the cases of women who had remained unmarried. They would return home having reached an age when finding employment in Britain was proving difficult.

The general reason for women migrating to Britain was the common belief that they would have little trouble finding work. From 1840 onwards a significant number of middle class women found employment in Britain as teachers, it being customary for the upper classes in many European countries to converse in German, French and English. Therefore, the initial reason for moving to Britain was to learn the English language with the intention of improving chances of employment on their return to Germany, where there was a surplus of school teachers, or to find a position as a governess in Britain and teach the German language to upper class children. Those who could give music tuition as well as lessons in drawing and painting obtained the best positions with the highest salaries.[9] Even though problems arose in the late nineteenth century with the opening of secondary schools for girls, the demand for governesses did not entirely disappear.

The German Teachers' Association, founded in 1883, filled various positions both in families and schools, although it was considered advisable to gain experience teaching families before facing a classroom of children. In addition, it also supplied staff – both male and female teachers – in a variety of positions. 'Superior Visiting Tutors' in the areas around London, for example, were highly successful in tutoring pupils for exams. Tutoring was also given during school holidays to students with learning difficulties. In cases of prejudice against foreigners, German women would often teach children in their own homes.

Even though working conditions were known to be unsatisfactory and the social position of a governess in Britain was inferior to that in Germany, most German governesses who wanted to work abroad preferred to go to England due to the fact that Queen Victoria employed a German governess for her children and she herself was brought up by a German governess. It has to be said that most German governesses in England did not lead comfortable lives, either from a financial or social point of view. Those who could not teach music often had difficulty in finding a job, which would usually be secured through an agency. Work in schools was poorly paid and any woman over thirty had difficulty in obtaining a position at all. In an essay on German women employed as a governess, an observer wrote:

> In Germany, the governess is accustomed to an easy-going life; she is like the eldest daughter of the house and generally made welcome everywhere. Here she is relegated to the schoolroom which is her kingdom indeed, but also her island, where she has to live as it were, in seclusion. Outside the schoolroom she has no rights. Her supper she has to eat in solitude within the same four walls, while she knows that the whole family are dining together comfortable downstairs, and that they will spend a cheerful, sociable evening afterwards in the drawing-room. This seems a heartless custom to be adopted by a people who pride themselves so much on their Christian love and charity.[10]

Another difficulty arose around the mid-nineteenth century when English parents wished to interview prospective governesses before signing a contract. This resulted in a large number of women crossing the channel on their own initiative and without having secured a position. This was the case of Dorette Mittendorf, a young girl who originated from north Germany and whose parents had died leaving her a small amount of money. With the sum of money, she successfully completed a teacher's training course and for a short while worked as a governess. Being a qualified teacher and having heard that teacher's wages were higher in England than in Germany, she decided to travel to England, stay with some relatives, and find work as a teacher. Even though she registered with employment agencies and advertised in a newspaper, nothing came of her attempts at finding a job. The big city frightened her; she was attacked, robbed and fell ill, and after a bad job experience her situation became desperate. The homes for governesses had no vacancies; her relatives couldn't support her and having run out of money she had nowhere to go. Eventually things changed for the better and she found good posts with the families of gentry. After about twenty years of teaching and governessing, her life took on a new purpose and in 1868 she opened a home for neglected small girls in North London. After she returned to Germany in 1889, the home was taken over by Dr Barnardo, the famous Irish philanthropist who was a friend of hers and the founder and director of homes for poor children.

Franziska Tiburtius was born in 1843. Unlike Dorette Mittendorf she was a more cheerful and optimistic young woman, having grown up in a large family. Dorette trained as a governess and, after gaining more experience, qualified as a teacher in 1868. Her aim was to become a headmistress. To improve her English and gain a broader outlook on life she went to England and, having no difficulty in finding a job, chose to work in a Suffolk rectory teaching German, French, music, geography and history to four girls between the ages of twelve and nineteen. The parents of her pupils were eccentric but friendly people and, while living in their house, she decided to go to Zurich and study medicine. Like many other governesses, Franziska commentated in her writings on her life in England. She found 'keeping Sunday' unacceptable, loathed the English weather in often poorly heated houses, and found the rigid, typically British class distinction ridiculous. She compared the rector in whose house she was living with German parsons and found him lacking in knowledge and theological learning to an astonishing degree. Franziska found the English teaching method of mainly memorizing from books old fashioned, but was impressed with the English principles of character building. In comparison to Germany, where obedience and humility were taught, she found the individuality of a child better respected in England and a sense of responsibility better encouraged. English children were more strenuous, having acquired a self confidence and self respect that German children sometimes lacked. Another difference she described was the appearance of teenage girls; in 1870, English children and upper class teenagers wore their hair loose and dressed attractively in vivid colours, in contrast to the conservative attire of young Germans.

One of the leading organisations giving support to German teachers was Gordon House – a philanthropic-funded institution that had the purpose of finding situations in service, as well as providing German women in London with accommodation if needed. The Association of German Governesses, founded in 1876 by forty-six members, was closely connected with the General Association of Female Teachers in Germany and in England. The association was supported through fundraising, as well as by the German embassy, German merchants, the German Kaiser and members of the British high society. It was able to open a home for governesses and other facilities and secured about 200 positions each year.[11]

Women's Rights

An illustrious and resolute German-born suffragette was Katherina Schafer, born 1871 in Westphalia, Germany, who came to England at the age of eighteen to escape her violent father and to join her sister, Dora.

After learning English, she became a successful actress and changed her name to Kitty Marion. In 1908, Kitty Marion began to take a keen interest in politics and became an active member of the Women's Social and Political Union (WSPU). One year later, she played a major part in forming the Actresses' Franchise League – a suffrage organisation aimed at improving female education, campaigning for women's rights and against the 'casting couch' tactics of music hall agents. Still continuing her career as an actress and music hall star, Kitty was arrested on numerous occasions for taking part in demonstrations.

On one occasion, she described being arrested outside the House of Commons and recalled:

> Two policemen, one on each arm, quite unnecessarily pinching and bruising the soft underarm, with the third often pushing at the back, would run us along and fling us, causing most women to be thrown to the ground.

Having then become a radical suffragette, Kitty took part in numerous actions such as breaking windows, throwing stones, and setting fire to empty buildings, for which she was sent to prison. Once in prison, she would go on a hunger strike and was force-fed. One of her comrades, Mary Leigh, describes the experience of this type of punishment.

> The wardress forced me onto the bed and two doctors inserted a nasal tube, which was two yards long with a funnel at the end. There was a glass junction in the

The German-born actress and suffragette Katherina Maria Schafer, known as Kitty Marion. (© National Portrait Gallery, London).

middle to see if the liquid was passing. The end was put up the right and left nostril on alternative days. The sensation was most painful – the drums of the ears seemed to be bursting and there was a horrible pain in the throat and the breast. The tube was pushed down twenty inches. I was pinned down on the bed by the wardresses, one doctor holding the funnel end and the other doctor forcing the other end up the nostrils. The one holding the funnel end poured the liquid down – about a pint of mile... egg and milk is sometimes used.

On 4 August 1914, when England declared war on Germany, Emmeline Pankhurst announced that all militants had to 'fight for their country as they fought for the vote'. Although Kitty Marion resumed her career as an actress, she still continued to campaign for women's rights.

Having been born in Germany, the government decided to deport her from Britain as with all female foreigners who could not be interned, but eventually allowed her to go the United States instead, where she continued campaigning for women's rights. Kitty Marion died in New York City in October 1944.[12]

Literature

One of Germany's most famous literary and intellectual icons, Johann Wolfgang von Goethe, whose influence upon European culture has been immense, could not by any means be described as a migrant. He maintained close connections with Britain and kept himself informed upon the reception of his work. Even though his command of the English language was never very strong, he was able to read magazines and newspapers as well as the literary works of his contemporaries, such as Sir Walter Scott and Lord Byron. He also corresponded with numerous British writers, such as William Taylor (1765–1836), who translated some of Goethe's work with the intention of making German literature more popular in Britain. Taylor's *Historic Survey on German Literature* was not entirely successful in Britain, compared to in Scotland, where a great deal of interest was shown in the German language, especially after Goethe's work had been published abroad, making him a European celebrity.

By the late eighteenth century Edinburgh had become a centre of language learning and the young Scottish poet (Sir) Walter Scott took lessons in German. Soon he was able to read works by Schiller and Goethe and in 1799 attempted a translation of Goethe's *Goetz von Berlichingen*. Although his command of German was not altogether perfect either, he successfully reproduced the spirit of Goethe's play. The ideas that Scott encountered in this drama of chivalric values confronted by political change and historical revolutions, found their way into his own writing which inspired his growing success. Although German plays were still open to ridicule, the impulse that this translation gave to Scott's own literary efforts was of singular importance. In later years the mutual appreciation between Scott and Goethe even induced them to borrow from each other's work (Goethe himself borrowed from other writers and saw no problem with that, although he did occasionally criticize the adaption of his 'borrowed' characters in Scott's work).

Scott's biographer, J. G. Lockhart, was struck by the 'many points of resemblance between the tone and spirit of Goethe's delineation and that afterwards adopted by [Scott] in some of the most remarkable of his original works'. Examples are given in the death scene in *Marmion* and the storm in *Ivanhoe*. Goethe used a scene from *Kenilworth* in *Faust Part Two,* while Scott himself used a detail from *Egmont* in the same novel.

The other major British writer and poet of this period was Byron (1788–1824) who, although almost forty years his junior, corresponded regularly with Goethe. Their friendship attracted a considerable amount of attention at that time and, although they didn't always see eye to eye, they were greatly inspired by each other's work. On Byron's death in 1824 Goethe remarked,

> The English … may think of Byron as they please; but this is certain, that they can show no poet who is to be compared to him. He is different from all the others, and, for the most part, greater.

New attention was given to Goethe after his death in 1832, due to further translations of his work, especially by Thomas Carlyle (1795–1881), which inspired the work of many more writers, especially Marian Evans, better known as George Eliot (1819–1880). Together with her life companion George Henry Lewes (1817–1878) she wrote the biography *Life of Goethe*. Her acquaintance with Goethe's work and her understanding of German literature also found their echo in some of her novels – most particularly *The Mill on the Floss* and *Daniel Deronda*, which draw on Goethe's *Die Wahlverwandschaften, Faust* and *Wilhelm Meister*.

Goethe's works mirrored the upheavals and developments on the continent which did not necessarily have the same affect on Britain. He was not only a serious poet, dramatist and ground breaking novelist, he was also a short story writer, essayist, diarist and critic. At the same time, he was a scientist working in optics, anatomy and natural history as well as being a highly respected botanist, horticulturist and inspired landscape designer. His genius was so many-sided that is was difficult for British readers and critics – apart from a discerning few – to see him as a whole.[13]

The British Goethe Society was founded in 1886 with the aim to promote the study of Goethe's work and thoughts. In the first year, membership reached nearly 300 and branches were formed in Manchester, Oxford, Birmingham and Glasgow. By the 1890s, membership went into steep decline so that the society's scope was extended to other fields of German literature, keeping Goethe as the central figure. In 1899, celebrations for Goethe's 150th birthday were held at Her Majesty's Theatre in London, with performances from Beethoven, Wagner, Liszt and songs written by Goethe himself. The Goethe Society has since become a world wide institution with lectures and discussions on Germanic Studies.

5

GERMAN INSTITUTIONS

Political Organisations

The liberal political system in Britain attracted those who had suffered repression in their own country, especially after unsuccessful attempts to form working class movements in Germany. German trade unions in Britain became legalised with British unions in 1824. They grew according to the type of trade they represented; in many cases they became more powerful in the exploitive trades, such as hairdressing and waiting.

The founding of political organisations such as the socialist and communist German Workers Education began around 1840, with the aim of educating workers to improve their social position. Other political movements were founded often with very few members. They represented the interests of working classes in industrial Britain and often involved workers of mixed nationalities, which also included the British.

The mid-nineteenth century brought great political changes in Europe, which affected Britain in as much as political refugees were now entering the country, along with the attitudes they brought with them. Their ideologies varied from 'liberal' to 'communist' with a number of sub-divisions, which included German intellectuals who had taken part in the 1848 March Revolution – one of many revolutions that had spread throughout Europe demanding liberal reform. Groups of students, intellectuals and workers demanded reforms and national unity.[1] In March 1848 they gathered in Berlin to present their demands to King Friedrich Wilhelm IV (the brother of Wilhelm I), who was said to have been indecisive and politically misinformed. The monarch, who was surprised at the intensity of the demonstration, agreed to the demonstrators' demands, which included parliamentary elections, a constitution, and freedom of the press. He also promised that 'Prussia was to be merged forthwith into Germany' (Germany still consisted of a group of independent states led by Prussia, which supplied the German monarchy). Because further demonstrations were put down by charging soldiers, a mass demonstration took place on 18 March in Berlin, which resulted in hundreds of civilian deaths after street barricades had been erected and the fighting began. Thirteen hours later troops were ordered to retreat.

After Friedrich Wilhelm had reassured the public that their demands would be met, a German National Assembly of deputies from various German states was democratically elected. Known sarcastically as the 'professor's parliament' due to the fact that it was without working class representation, it proved itself ineffective, being unable to pass resolutions, which usually dissolved into endless debate.

King Friedrich Wilhelm IV then imposed a monarchist constitution. This took effect on 5 December 1848. Otto von Bismarck was elected to the first Landtag – later to be known as The Frankfurt National Assembly – which was also unable to agree on national policies and proved incapable of governing the country. The National Assembly was dissolved on 31 May 1849, thus demonstrating the failure of The March Revolution to enforce a democratic government in a united Germany.[2]

Many revolutionists sought refuge in England. This resulted in a transfer of German political organisations to England, which clearly attracted newcomers and introduced another type of (political) chain migration. Despite Britain's liberal atmosphere and the shelter given to intellectual outcasts, dissidents and revolutionaries as well as prominent socialists such as Karl Marx and Friedrich Engels were shocked at the unacceptable condition of factory workers.

Marx, a journalist who later studied political economy and philosophy, spent much of his adult life in London. Friedrich Engels was a German philosopher, social scientist, journalist and businessman. Together they founded the Marxist theory and, in 1845, published *The Condition of the Working-class in England*, based on personal observations and research made in Manchester. Marx and Engels shared the same social and reformative views and began spreading their ideas on 'Revolutionary Proletarian Socialism', which later became known as communism; the Communist League, founded in London, was to be followed by hundreds of German political organisations. They also published various works, the most famous of these being the 1848 pamphlet 'The Communist Manifesto'.[3]

Exiles pursued their political activities as journalists and authors who wrote for political magazines and German newspapers. Other political organisations among many were the 'German Workers Educational Association Club' in Soho with another branch in the East End. Another splitter of these clubs was the 'Gruppe Autonomie' which published its own newspaper, *Die Autonomie*. The 'Communist League and the Communistic Society for the Training of Artisans' had connections with international organisations such as the 'Socialist League' and the 'Freedom League'. These political organisations also offered social activities to their members, including further education for workers as well as political discussions that continued until the outbreak of the First World War.[4] Although churches remained the stronghold of German ethnicity, German newspapers, which existed in Britain during the nineteenth century, were a source of information for ethnic minorities in general. For the migrants, they were a suitable way of finding things out about their new country, understandably written in their own language. German language trade journals sponsored by trade organisations helped employers find work. They advertised vacant situations, published articles as guidelines for new arrivals and information relating to rules and regulations of employment in Britain. The press also conveyed the latest news from their homeland, which kept them in touch with political developments and maintained the contact between their old and new countries.

The number of German newspapers printed in London during the nineteenth century is estimated to have exceeded 100. Only one newspaper – *The Manchester Nachrichten* – was printed outside the capital and published from 1910 to 1912 due to the lack of markets in smaller communities that would only support a few hundred copies. The newspapers covered the daily news and political developments, as well as social and religious issues. Many printed a few hundred copies and only appeared for a limited period.

The longest running newspapers in Victorian and Edwardian London still in print on the outbreak of the First World War, were *Die Finanzchronik* – a financial weekly journal; *the Londoner General Anzeiger* printed twice-weekly and concentrated on major British news stories; and the *Londoner Zeitung*, originally known as *Hermann*, which was originally aimed at the German exile community but widened its scope after changing its name.[5] A political newspaper was the *Kosmos*, which appeared in 1851 with only three editions. It was edited by Ernst Haug, a former Austrian officer who had taken part in the 1848 revolutions. The paper covered Austria, Germany and Italy and had the support of many other refugees. *Der Deutsche Eidgenosse* first appeared in March 1865, with the explicit aim of overthrowing the tyranny in Germany. Articles written by liberal exiles in England were published every two weeks, until the newspaper closed after the unification of the German states and the formation of the German Empire in 1871.

Social Organisations

The growth of the German population during the eighteenth century led to the development of more German social and cultural organisations that differed according to class. Considering the fact that approximately 50 per cent of Germans in Great Britain had settled in London (about 25,000), it is hardly surprising that German clubs for social activities, known as the *Vereins*, were also centred in London (as were most ethnic organisations), as well as in the larger cities such as Bradford, Manchester and Glasgow.

Before the advent of trade unions, similar organisations to the *Vereins* served Germans of a particular occupation, such as the 'German Evangelical Seemansmission', which was one of the largest German philanthropic organisations in Britain and originated from various independent missions stationed in British ports with the intention of caring for and protecting German sailors while visiting England. The *Vereins* catered predominantly for the wealthier upper and middle classes, having been formed by people of similar interests and social standing. A British satirist remarked:

> Wherever a dozen Germans meet there is sure to be a *Verein* of some sort, which is not a club, nor is it a union as we understand, but it partakes of both and is something more besides.[6]

This description of ethnic groups in Britain refers to the hundreds which existed throughout the country during the Victorian and Edwardian years.

One of the more outstanding *Verein* was the 'German Gymnastic Club' or '*Turnverein*'. It was founded at the Schiller Festival in 1859 to celebrate the centenary of the poet's birth and opened with a large gymnasium and a very spacious concert hall. By 1862 membership had reached 1,000 gymnasts and supporters, in a building now familiar to many rail travellers as they emerge from the new entrance to St Pancras International, opposite King's Cross.

German gymnastics became extremely popular among Victorian Londoners and the newly built gymnasium was, in 1866, one of three venues in London to host the first ever national Olympian Games of the modern era. The National Olympian Association, formed by the wealthy businessman Ernst Ravenstein of the German Gymnasium, was the forerunner of the modern-day British Olympic Association and helped increase awareness of physical education during the Victorian era. Ultimately, the British would adopt a form of gymnastics that had its roots in Stockholm rather than Berlin, partly because German gymnastics were geared towards military needs and also because a gymnasium fitted out for German gymnastics cost six times more than a Swedish one. The building, which was restored in 2008, still features the laminated timber roof, which is a German invention, and is still fitted with the original hooks used for suspending the gymnasts' ropes.

There were also gymnastic clubs outside the capital along with a range of other '*Vaterländische Vereine*', such as the '*Schillerverein*' in Bradford, which was founded in 1861 by wealthy German-Jewish wool merchants for the purpose of 'sociable meetings with fellow businessmen'. Another typical German *Verein* was the '*Lieder Tafel*' or '*Liederkranz*', which were social gatherings for a song – mostly traditional German songs sung in (a male) chorus around a festive table (*Tafel*), usually in the reserved room of a German restaurant in a jovial atmosphere depending on the amount of beer already consumed. The Deutsche Club organised social and informative gatherings and was present in almost every city with a sizeable German community.

The German Athenaeum was the most select and exclusive of all German societies in London and attracted the elite of the German population. It was founded in 1869 and described as a social rallying point for the furthering of art and science with exhibitions, musical evenings and lectures on scientific topics.

Philanthropic organisations played the most important role in the creation of a German 'community'. Wealthy Germans assisted their poorer countrymen, therefore maintaining class divisions, but on the whole, philanthropic entrepreneurs such as Jacob Moser, who had made a fortune in the Bradford wool trade, contributed enormous sums of money to charitable organisations in Bradford with the intention of supporting factory workers and educating their children.[7]

But one of the most effective and significant innovations to be established in Great Britain was The National Insurance Act of 1911, which is often regarded as the foundation of modern social welfare in the United Kingdom; a national contributory program for manual workers as a move to weaken the growing strength of labour unions. This had been greatly influenced by Germany's Health Insurance Act of 1883, which was introduced by Chancellor Otto von Bismarck. He had been convinced that a health, accident, old age and unemployment insurance law could solve many social problems and win the good will of labourers. Although this contributory programme became a model for many other countries, it was abandoned by Britain in 1948 in favour of the first government scheme for free and universal entitlement to publicly provided medical care.[8]

Religion and Charity

In 1891 Germans formed the largest continental grouping in Britain. By 1911 the population had increased to 53,324 – the peak figure before 1914. Migrants who entered the country during the nineteenth century probably exceeded the entire total that had entered the country during the previous thousand years.

We have already seen that the eighteenth and nineteenth centuries saw a huge influx of German-speaking immigrants from all sectors of society, attracted by a growing demand for skilled workers in Britain's rapidly growing industrial cities. Although large numbers of German migrants in Britain were merchants and skilled workers, a great mass of migrants belonged to the lower classes. The poorer peasants forced into migration through hunger were willing to take on menial jobs and work as labourers in the hope of gaining certain skills, which would enable them to improve their standard of living. Having started as kitchen hands, they would later become waiters or house servants. Many became successful businessmen and highly respected entrepreneurs, which they would never have achieved in their homeland.

But not all migrants were successful in their new country and those who worked for their own countrymen were often exploited and poorly paid. They remained at the bottom of the social scale having failed to achieve their goal, often through illness or redundancy. Many became paupers, dependent upon the numerous ethnic charity organisations run by the German community and the Lutheran Church, for foreigners in distress. These charities were usually based in London, as it had the largest German community. Branches opened in other main areas of German population that had developing communities such as Hull, Glasgow, Leeds, Liverpool, Bradford, Huddersfield, Manchester and Liverpool.

One of the three major charities that existed was 'The Mission Among the German Poor in London' – a Christian mission established in 1849. They visited underprivileged

German families in London, mainly in Soho. In 1874, they were recorded as having paid 4,768 house visits. Their purpose, besides offering Christian advice and spreading the Word of God, was to educate the German poor in the east of London, where they set up a day school in Whitechapel.[9]

Another major charity was 'The German Society of Benevolence', founded in 1817, to established funds for members who had fallen into distress. Within a period of eleven years, those who received financial assistance rose from 903 in 1871 to a peak of over 4,000. The charity supported old people who could no longer work and provided them with pensions. They often donated money to individual applicants in cases of short-term relief from financial difficulties and in some cases people received money for a return ticket to Germany.

'The Society of Friends of Foreigners in Distress' was perhaps the more important organisation because of its large resources. It assisted all immigrants in difficulty. The type of assistance offered included medical and legal aid, as well as clothing, lodgings, the search for employment and financial support. These institutions were also supported by several European monarchies as well as the British Royal Family, the Archbishop of Canterbury, other well-known British donors.

German charities supported the 'German Farm Colony in Libury Hall' situated in Ware in Hertfordshire, 30 miles from London. It opened in 1900 with a substantial grant from the Schröder Banking House, which had given numerous philanthropic donations to Germans in Britain before the First World War.

The colony had three aims: to provide, under Christian influence, temporary work, shelter, board and lodging for German-speaking unemployed and destitute men of whatever creed who were able and willing to work, thus giving them a fresh start in life; to assist those anxious to return to their home to earn sufficient money for that purpose; and to suppress as far as possible habitual begging with its concomitant moral degradation.

Those in the farm colony had to work between ten and twelve hours per day, for which they obtained a small wage, with the exception of German-speaking pensioners over sixty who were offered permanent residence. Their numbers fluctuated between about fifty shortly after its foundation and 150 shortly before the outbreak of the First World War. During the first five years of its existence, a total of 2,500 men were admitted to the colony, a figure that had risen further by the end of 1913 to 6,941 men, including 5,073 Germans.[10]

Several German charities that came into existence in the early twentieth century were not only supported by the British Royal Family, but also 'The Kaiser Wilhelm II Fund for the Relief of Needy and Deserving Persons of German Nationality'. One of these institutions was The German Hospital, opened in 1845 in Hackney, to assist the Germans who 'chiefly belong to the humbler classes of society and of whom there are, at all times, hundreds among them in want of hospital relief', but who had difficulties in obtaining hospital care at English institutions. Here it can be mentioned that members of hospital staff were expected to have a command of the German language. The hospital survived on huge donations, which enabled the opening of a convalescent home.

In 1911, and with the backing of Bruno Schröder (Schröder Banking House), a German Old People's Home was opened in Clapton. Another institution was The German Orphanage and School situated in Dalston and founded through the Kaiser Wilhelm Foundation in 1879, which accommodated up to forty children. Independent German schools also existed, catering for the sons and daughters of the German middle classes. The German-English Boys School opened in Brixton in 1878. A similar institution existed in London in the form of German Higher Daughters School. Both schools offered 'the children of Germans in England a thorough, intellectual, spiritual and character-building education'.

In the first half of the eighteenth century there were around 4,000 congregants in London's German churches. The most famous of these was St George's German Lutheran Church in Alie Street, founded in 1762/3, which is the oldest surviving German church-building in Britain. It originally served the German community in the area of the flourishing sugar trade.

The principal founder of the church was the sugar-refiner Dederich Beckmann, who put £650 towards the £1,802 10s 9d cost of the lease and construction of the church. His nephew, Dr Gustavus Anthony Wachsel, was the first pastor. He got into conflict with trustees and elders by preaching sermons in English and introducing English hymns, English singers and musical instruments into the choir. Performances were said to have been accompanied by the eating of 'apples, oranges, nuts, etc, as in a theatre', leading the church to obtain the name 'St George's Playhouse.'

By 1815 there were already five Protestant churches, one Roman Catholic Church and at least four synagogues in London. By 1905 the Hamburg Lutheran Church in Hackney possessed one of the largest congregations with an attendance of 218 worshipers, second only to St Mary's in Cleveland Street, St Pancras, with an attendance of 281. St Mary's possessed the oldest German school in London, ran a Society for German and Swiss Girls, and gathered books for a library. The Women's Committee, like many other parishes of German church communities, aimed at caring for the poor and old. These were financed by annual fundraising evenings.[11]

In the type of occupation where exploitation was customary – as in the sugar and clothing industries where workers were poor, uneducated and seldom remained for great lengths of time – the support given by religious missions and local churches was imperative. Many other London church parishes organised benevolent, educational, and women's organisations, and the schools they ran offered free schooling to children from poorer families, again with donations from the Schröder family (Schröder Banking House) who played a major role in philanthropic activity among the Germans in Victorian and Edwardian Britain. In religion, local communities were served according to population. In most industrial cities of Britain, one church would often serve the community as a whole.

In Manchester, one of the three Protestant churches that existed at the end of the nineteenth century served a distinctly middle class community of German businessmen and merchants. The German Mission Church served poorer members and was financed by subscriptions. A day school was later opened in a new building aimed at bringing destitute children 'to a point where the boys could work as errand boys or in warehouses and the girls could become housemaids in German or English middle-class families'.

In the late nineteenth century, a total of 154 Germans merchants in Manchester as well as a large number of academics and well-known nineteenth-century figures such as the composer Sir Charles Halle and Franz Liszt (although Franz Liszt was a prolific Hungarian-Austrian musician) were members of this lively German community. Not only did a wealthy middle class represent the large German population, but also poorer classes – many described as 'adventurers' and others as exiled revolutionaries. As in most northern towns there was a floating population of criminals and petty thieves who would move from one charity to the other. In 1862, The Society for the Relief of Distressed Foreigners is recorded as having given active support to 309 German families who were at the bottom of the social scale.

The German Lutheran Church in Liverpool, founded in the early nineteenth century, succeeded the Bethel Union, which had held church services in German onboard a ship docked in the Mersey. Greatly appreciated by German-speaking crews was the City Mission, which opened in 1862. The Lutheran Church helped passengers who were attracted by the opportunities a rapidly expanding industrial city had to offer.

Many migrants on their way to the New World left their ships in Liverpool in the hope of finding work and accommodation nearer home; support was given to trans-migrants stopping-over. Charity work and assisting the poor was another important aspect of the Lutheran Church. A school was opened in 1865 that taught the German language to children visiting British schools, as well as singing and Bible Studies. A Women's Mission collected clothes for the needy and in 1890 a German Christian Waiters' Society was founded. In general, the church acted as a central organ for the maintenance of German culture for all ages and social standing, financed through yearly subscriptions, donations from wealthy Liverpool Germans and church collections.[12]

The German Lutheran Church in Hull, founded in 1840, also supported visiting German sailors and trans-migrants to America, Canada and Australia on short stop-overs in British ports before continuing their journeys. The more middle class congregation of German businessmen, tradesmen, shop owners and refugees remained smaller in number than in Liverpool's church community, although it still pursued similar benevolent activities, which included a school to accommodate around fifty children.

In Sunderland, the German church, which began holding services around 1860, catered mostly for German pork butchers and musicians. Once again, a donation given by Baron Schröder (Schröder Banking House) enabled church services to be conducted by Sunderland's resident minister for the benefit of German congregations in north-eastern Britain, including South Shields, Newcastle, Hartlepool and Middlesbrough.

The Bradford Lutheran Church was founded in 1877. In 1882 the growing congregation purchased a school, which it transformed into a church with the financial support of not only local Germans, but the German Kaiser and the King of Bavaria. The mainly middle class congregation had grown from approximately 75 members to over 150 members by 1889. In 1913 membership declined to around 50 and only 14 pupils attended the school. Due to Bradford's wealth, it being 'the wool capital of the world', members of the congregation were predominantly middle class citizens – mostly German wool merchants – who made generous contributions to the church, although there seems to have been less need for charitable work in Bradford than in other parts of the country.[13]

German/Jewish Communities

The first records of Jews having settled in England go back to William the Conqueror in 1066, who is said to have brought a group of Sephardic Jews from France to undertake the task of collecting coins for dues and taxes on behalf of the crown. Their presence continued until they were expelled in 1290 by King Edward I. After the 'Edict of Expulsion' there was no Jewish community until in 1656 when Rabbi Manasseh ben Israel of Holland persuaded Oliver Cromwell to allow a colony of Sephardic Jews to settle in London. By 1690 increasing numbers had entered Britain from Poland, Germany and Holland, so that by 1692 the first synagogue was established in London despite surreptitious misgivings.

Towards the end of the eighteenth century a number of synagogues opened in London, dedicated to various studies according to the religious habits of different Jewish communities, including one for German Jews known as the Hamburg or Hambros.[14] This caused a great deal of wrangling on rabbinical authority until it was agreed that the main synagogue should be The Great Synagogue of London, built around 1690 at Duke's Place, north of Aldgate in London, which was later followed by a new building in 1722.

As their numbers and resources grew, the congregation built a third version on the site between 1788 and 1790.

Britain's reputation for religious tolerance continued to attract Jews from Germany and other Eastern European countries. Places of worship catered for migrants from all parts of the world and each synagogue, supported by the major synagogues, assumed responsibility for

The Bevis Marks Synagogue is the oldest synagogue in the United Kingdom and is located off Bevis Marks in the city of London. It was built in 1701 and is the only synagogue in Europe that has held regular services continuously for more than 300 years. (© Edwardx – licensed under the Creative Commons Attribution-Share Alike).

relieving its poorer members. During the eighteenth century, few Jews were attracted to the Midlands and the North but preferred to settle in the coastal towns as a direct consequence of the expansion of the Royal Navy during that century. This provided opportunities for small commercial activities, which served both the civilian and naval populations in the ports. Jews were also prominent as outfitters for sailor's clothing and chandlers for sailing gear and as naval agents whereby they provided sailors with financial services such as goods on credit of money loans. They also exchanged foreign currencies, sold cheap watches and other jewellery to ship-bound sailors who were not permitted to go ashore for fear they might desert. By the end of the eighteenth century similar business ventures had spread into provincial cities such as Birmingham, Liverpool, Norwich and Sunderland.

By 1780, fifteen Jewish families had settled in Manchester and by 1815 there was already a synagogue and Jewish cemetery for a growing community. During the first half of the nineteenth century a further influx of Jewish merchants and poorer Jews from East Prussia and Russia arrived in Manchester, which had now developed into an already large, closely knit Jewish community with a lively assortment of social, religious and educational activities.[15] Like Manchester, Bradford also had a wealthy German/Jewish community with little mention of lower and humble classes, probably due to the philanthropic activities of wealthy merchants such as Jacob Moser, Charles Semon and Jacob Behrens. One commentator writing in the *Daily Mail* of 29 June 1909 claimed, 'I have never seen so many German names in one community outside Germany', but that 'the German colony is remarkably small. There is no competition at all from German labour, and indeed very little of it in the professional classes'.

Referring particularly to the middle class German immigrants, a more recent commentator has written that, 'their influence was out of all proportion to their numbers' as reflected 'in the architecture of parts of central Bradford and the rich cultural heritage they bestowed on the city'.

Although German/Jewish communities developed their own institutions, which included hospitals, free schools, and benevolent societies, the most significant characteristic of English Jewish religious life in the eighteenth century was its laxity, especially among the very rich and the very poor. Wealthy Jews acquired country homes and estates and practised the same aristocratic lifestyle as their Gentile contemporaries. The poor – by far the largest section of the community – underwent a similar transformation by neglecting the rites and customs of their religion or, in the case of criminals, living outside any religious framework whatsoever. By the end of the century, synagogue attendance and the general level of religious practice in England had dropped to a markedly lower level than elsewhere in Europe.[16] This might have been partly due to the fact that legal disabilities faced all non-members of the Church of England. Unable to swear a Christological oath or take the sacrament in the Church of England, they were not allowed to serve in Parliament, vote in parliamentary elections (in theory – in fact they did vote), hold municipal office, be called to the Bar, obtain a naval commission or matriculate, or take a degree at Oxford and Cambridge. For many Jews, this meant exclusion from the freedom of the City, rendering them unable to operate a retail business within its boundaries.[17] Indeed, it was not until 1829 that Jews were finally allowed to sit in Parliament. Benjamin Disraeli was the first Jewish-born Member of Parliament and Britain's Prime Minister from 1874 to 1880, although his father left Judaism after a dispute at his synagogue and Benjamin became an Anglican at the age of twelve.

From the beginning of the Industrial Revolution, a system of Jewish merchants with worldwide contacts played an important role in the development of business and commerce in Great Britain with the rest of the world. This would continue to expand throughout the century until the First World War.

6

GERMAN INGENUITY

The development of steam-powered machinery, new methods of mass production and rapid growth of transport systems, as well as ingenious discoveries in the fields of science and inventive technology, constituted the Industrial Revolution. It brought vast social and economic changes due to the rapid growth of industrial strength during the eighteenth and nineteenth centuries, not only in Great Britain but also in Europe.

Industrial cities in Britain involved in the textile industry – such as Yorkshire's wool industry in Bradford and Lancashire's cotton industry in Manchester – attracted numerous Germans involved in production and export. Towards the end of the nineteenth century, Jewish bankers transferred their businesses from Frankfurt or Berlin to London and a large movement of clerks began opening their own businesses.

From the first half of the nineteenth century onwards, German universities and *Technische Hochschulen* had been traditionally seen as the most important element in a powerful education system to meet the demands of industry and bring forth a new generation of scientists and entrepreneurs in Europe. After 1850, the states of Germany had rapidly become industrialized with particular strengths in coal, iron and later steel, chemicals and railways; although the easy-going life style and opportunities offered in Britain's growing economy were also an attractive alternative to young academics, merchants and tradesmen. There are many examples of individuals involved in banking and industry who migrated to Britain.

Here we can mention some of the more outstanding personalities, such as Friedrich Christian Accum or Frederick Accum (1769–1838), a German chemist born in Bückenburg, Schaumburg-Lippe near Hanover. In 1793 he went to London as an apprentice to the German branch of the Brande family in Arlington Street, who were apothecaries to George III. Later, he pursued scientific and medical studies at the School of Anatomy in Great Windmill Street as well as manufacturing and selling a variety of chemicals and laboratory equipment. He also gave fee-based public lectures in practical chemistry and collaborated with research efforts at numerous other institutes of science.

His most important achievements included advances in the field of gas lighting. To replace the costly use of candles or oil lamps, Accum became involved in the production of gas using the poisonous by-products of coal, tar and sulphur compounds, which had been responsible for extensive environmental damage. This revolutionised industrial lighting, especially in textile factories and later in urban life. Together with another German chemist, Frederick Winzer from Brunswick, they established the first gas plant in the history of gaslight – the Gas Light & Coke Company, which eventually became British Gas.

Satirical print of Friedrich Accum lecturing on food adulteration at the Surrey Institution. Artist, Thomas Rowlandson, title *Chemical Lectures*.

    The beginning of the nineteenth century also saw a rapid increase in the industrial preparation and packaging of foods. Instead of between local farmers and townspeople, the production and distribution of food had become a centralized factory process and the drastic increase of additives used in these processes, a serious health concern. Newly discovered chemicals and the absence of laws moderating their use had made it possible for unscrupulous merchants to use them, so boosting their profits at the expense of public health. Frederick Accum was the first to publicly proclaim the hazards of this practice and reached a wide audience with his concerns. This ground breaking work marked the beginning of an awareness of need for food safety. He informed the reader upon every type of additive, from less dangerous substances such as ground dried peas in coffee, to dangerous contamination by truly poisonous substances. One of many examples was the high lead content in Spanish olive oil caused by the lead used in containers to clear the oil. Accum recommended using oil from other countries such as France and Italy where this was not practiced.

    In 1820 Accum began the struggle against harmful food additives with his book, *A Treatise on Adulterations of Food and Culinary Poisons. There is Death in the Pot.* He warned against bright green sweets sold by travelling merchants in the streets of London as the colour was produced with 'sapgreen', a colorant with high copper content. 'Vinegar', he explained to his readers, 'was frequently mixed with sulphuric acid in order to increase its acidity'. With particular attention to beer, he introduced the subject with the comment: 'Malt beverages, and especially port, the preferred drink of the inhabitants of London and other large cities, is among the items which are most frequently adulterated in the course of supply'. He claimed that English beer was occasionally mixed with molasses, honey, vitriol, pepper and even opium. Among the

A TREATISE

ON

ADULTERATIONS OF FOOD,

AND

Culinary Poisons,

EXHIBITING

THE FRAUDULENT SOPHISTICATIONS

OF

BREAD, BEER, WINE, SPIRITUOUS LIQUORS, TEA, COFFEE,

Cream, Confectionery, Vinegar, Mustard, Pepper, Cheese, Olive Oil, Pickles,

AND OTHER ARTICLES EMPLOYED IN DOMESTIC ECONOMY.

AND

Methods of Detecting them.

THERE IS
DEATH
IN THE POT
2 Kings C. IV.V 40

THE SECOND EDITION.

BY FREDRICK ACCUM,

Operative Chemist, Lecturer on Practical Chemistry, Mineralogy, and on Chemistry
applied to the Arts and Manufactures; Member of the Royal Irish Academy;
Fellow of the Linnæan Society; Member of the Royal Academy of
Sciences, and of the Royal Society of Arts of Berlin, &c. &c.

London:

SOLD BY LONGMAN, HURST, REES, ORME, AND BROWN,
PATERNOSTER ROW.
1820.

A Treatise on Adulterations of Food and Culinary Poisons by Friedrich Accum; *There is Death in the Pot* –The Wellcome Library, London. (© Available under Creative Commons Attribution only licence CC by 4.0).

most shocking habits during the French revolutionary wars, he pointed out, was the practice of adding fishberries, a poisonous alkaloid with stimulant properties to port.

In his book, he describes the simple techniques of the analytical chemistry he employed in discovering these facts, thereby making them more accessible to his readers with the intention of making every test repeatable in the simplest possible way by non-experts. Neither did he limit his campaign to simply exposing problems. At the end of every chapter he included names of merchants who had in years prior to 1820 been caught adulterating foodstuffs, so depriving them of business and thereby affecting the London economy.

His exposure of established malpractices within the food-processing industry earned him many enemies among the London food manufacturers. Frederick Accum left England and returned to Germany after a lawsuit was brought against him. He obtained a professorship at the Gewerbeinstitut and the Bauakademie – industrial institutions – in Berlin, where he lived for a further sixteen years until his death in 1838.[1]

The engineer Henry Gustav Simon (1835–1899) was born in Brieg, Silesia – then a province of Prussia. His father was a director at one of Germany's first railways, which sparked an inclination to study mechanics. In his teenage years Henry witnessed the revolutionary ferment of 1848 and gradually grew disillusioned with his native country. Despite arriving in Manchester in 1860 without a penny to his name, within seven years Henry had established himself as a consulting engineer with his own office and become a naturalised British citizen. By introducing a rolling flour milling plant for McDougall Brothers in Manchester, the likes of which he had seen working in Switzerland, Henry set in motion and guided the 'Rollermilling Revolution' – a mechanisation of the British flour milling system that revolutionised Great Britain's flour milling industry. His second son, Ernest Simon, went on to become the first baron of Wythenshawe.[2]

Another German scientist who came to England in 1862 was Ludwig Mond (1839–1909). He was born into a Jewish family in Kassel, Germany, and studied chemistry at the universities of Marburg and Heidelberg. Together with John Hutchinson he developed a method of recovering sulphur from the manufacture of soda. In 1872 he began to improve the process of manufacturing soda and, together with the industrialist John Brunner, he established the business Brunner Mond & Company. They built a soda-ash plant at Northwich in Cheshire, which was the start of what later became Imperial Chemical Industries (ICI). By 1880, the year he took British nationality, they had improved the production of soda, and within twenty years had become the world's largest producer. Mond later discovered nickel carbonyl, previously an unknown compound, which could be processed into pure nickel. For this he founded the Mond Nickel Company and imported from nickel mines in Canada to his works at Clydasch, near Swansea, Wales for final purification.[3]

The giant engineering firm Siemens traces its origins to the Siemens brothers; Werner (1816–1892), Wilhelm (1823–1883,) and Carl Heinrich (1829–1906), who originated from Lenthe near Hanover. Werner von Siemens was awarded his first Prussian patent in 1842, for an electrolytic method of gold and silver plating. His younger brother Wilhelm later successfully marketed this invention in Britain.

The Siemens brothers' primary interests, however, were in electric telegraphing and electric lighting. In 1846 Werner von Siemens improved the electrical pointer telegraph invented by the Englishman Charles Wheatstone. Siemens' device was superior to the apparatus in common use until then; it no longer worked like a clock mechanism but automatically controlled synchronization between the transmitter and the receiver – an entirely new solution in electric communications. Siemens then entrusted the construction of the telegraph to Johann Georg Halske, a precision mechanic who produced experimental equipment for many well-known scientists of the day, as well as prototypes for inventions in the fields of precision mechanics, physics, optics and chemistry.

The Telegraphen-Bauanstalt von Siemens & Halske, founded in 1847, developed the pointer telegraph and the first long-distance telegraph line in Europe. New business fields were opening up with the manufacture and laying of submarine telegraph cables. Wilhelm von Siemens' good contacts facilitated the difficult entry into the highly developed English telegraph market. Due to their success in the laying of the first deep-sea cable in the Mediterranean, they acted as personal advisers to the British government for all deep-sea cable projects. A major project undertaken by Siemens Brothers was the Indo-European telegraph, which ran through four different sovereign territories. In spite of considerable logistic, political and financial problems, the construction work was successfully concluded by the beginning of 1870 and on 12 April 1870 William (Wilhelm) Siemens created a sensation in London when he demonstrated sending and receiving an answer to a telegram on the 1,000-kilometre route between London and Calcutta within an hour. This line remained in operation until 1931 with only a single interruption due to the First World War. A telegraph link to America also commenced in 1874.

William also devoted himself intensively to scientific research. Together with his brother Friedrich, who spent several years in England, he developed a new process for the manufacture of steel, which became known as the Siemens-Martin process. In 1866 he built the Siemens Sample Steelworks in Birmingham and in 1867 registered his first patent for steel manufacture. Further patents followed and the Landore Siemens Steel Company near Swansea was also founded. Having become an established figure in English scientific circles, William became a member of the Royal Society in 1862 and in 1872 became founder and first president of the Society of Telegraph Engineers and Electricians. He also received honorary doctorates from a number of universities. A few months before his death in 1883, William was knighted Sir William Siemens by Queen Victoria.

Werner von Siemens' policy of further development in electrical engineering was to be continued after his death. In 1877 the first commercial telephone company entered the telephone business using the Siemens pipe as ringer and also fitted with devices built by Siemens. Siemens & Halske (S&H) was incorporated in 1897, and continued to merge part of its activities with other firms such as the Osram Lightbulb Company. New inventions connected with electric telegraphing and electric lighting soon produced a whole new programme of industrial products such as generators, motors, transformers and the complete assembly of power stations. During the 1920s and 1930s, S&H started to manufacture radios, television sets, electron microscopes and household appliances.[4]

In 1882 both Gottlieb Daimler (1834–1900) and his partner Wilhelm Maybach built the first automobile with an air-cooled one-cylinder high-speed internal-combustion engine. In 1885, they adapted an early model of the internal combustion engine and patented what is generally recognized as the prototype of the modern gas engine. The 1885 Daimler-Maybach engine was small and lightweight, and immediately put to use in the first motorcycle and the first motorboat. On March 8 1886, Daimler took a stagecoach (made by Wilhelm Wimpff & Son) and adapted it so that it could hold his engine. In the process, he ended up designing the world's first four-wheeled automobile.

It was capable of a top speed of 18 kilometres per hour. In 1890, Daimler founded the Daimler Motor Company in Cannstatt, near Stuttgart, to mass produce his designs. In 1899, Daimler asked Maybach to design a racing car, which was given the name *Mercedes*. In 1889 the car was based on a framework of light tubing with an engine in the rear, belt-driven wheels and steered by a tiller. The car proved to be of commercial

Gottlieb Daimler enjoying a ride in the back seat of his 'Motor Carriage', driven by his son Adolf. (With permission, Mercedes-Benz-Public Archives).

value, partly because it had four speeds, and in the following year the Daimler Motoren-Gesellschaft was founded. The British Daimler automobile was started as a manufactory licensed by the German company but later became independent when, in 1893, rights were purchased by Frederick Simms, who formed the 'Daimler Motor Syndicate'. In 1896 Simms and Harry Lawson moved into car production in the city of Coventry as the Daimler Motor Company.

In 1898 Daimler became the official transportation of royalty, after the Prince of Wales, later Edward VII, was given a ride in a Daimler by the Member of Parliament John Scott-Montagu who drove a Daimler into the yard of the British Parliament – the first motorized vehicle to be driven there. Every British monarch from Edward VII to our present Queen Elizabeth II was chauffeured in Daimler limousines, until Rolls-Royce was commissioned in 1950, putting Daimler into 'second place'.[4]

Carl von Linde (1842–1934), born in Berndorf (now Austria), was a German scientist and engineer who developed refrigeration through gas separation and liquefaction processes. These breakthroughs laid the backbone for the 1913 Nobel Prize in physics. He was the founder of what is now known as 'The Linde Group' – the world's largest industrial gases company – and supplied industrial gases as a profitable line of businesses. By 1880 the efficient new refrigeration technology offered big benefits to breweries and by 1890 Linde had sold 747 machines. In addition to the breweries, other uses for the new technology were found in slaughterhouses and cold storage facilities all over Europe.

In 1892 an order from the Guinness Brewery in Dublin for a Carbon Dioxide Liquefaction Plant drove Linde's research into the area of low-temperature refrigeration, and in 1894 he started work on a process for the liquefaction of air by first compressing it and then letting it expand rapidly, thereby cooling it. He then obtained oxygen and nitrogen from the liquid air by slow warming. He filed for patent protection of his process, which wasn't approved in the USA until 1903. In the early days of oxygen production, the biggest use by far for the gas was the oxyacetylene torch, invented in France in 1904, which revolutionized metal cutting and welding in the construction of ships, skyscrapers, and other iron and steel structures.

In addition to Linde's technical and engineering abilities, he was also a successful entrepreneur and formed international partnerships to exploit the value of his patents and knowledge through licensing arrangements. In 1906, Linde negotiated a stake in Brin's Oxygen Company (later The BOC Group) in exchange for patent rights and held a board position until 1914. In 1907 he formed the Linde Air Products Company in the USA, which passed through US government control to Union Carbide in the 1940s and went on to form today's Praxair. By 1910, co-workers including Carl's son Friedrich had developed the Linde Double Column Process – variants of which are still in common use today.

Shortly before the First World War, Linde transferred company operation to his sons Friedrich and Richard and his son-in-law Rudolf Wucherer. He still remained in close connection with his company until his death in Munich 1934, aged ninety-two years.[5]

Wilhelm Conrad Röntgen (1845–1923) was a German engineer and physicist who produced and detected, quite by accident, electromagnetic radiation in a wavelength range now known as X-rays or Röntgen-rays while experimenting with electrical currents through glass cathode ray tubes. He realised the significance of his discovery after taking an X-ray of his wife's hand, including her wedding ring; an achievement that earned him the first Nobel Prize in Physics in 1901, which he donated to his university. Like Pierre Curie, Röntgen refused to take out patents related to his discovery, claiming that mankind should benefit from his discovery – i.e. the ability to trace and diagnose problems in the human body, as well as use in industry and security.

7

THE LEGACY OF PRINCE ALBERT

Britain and Germany's Mutual Royal Family

The Act of Settlement of 1701 regulates the succession to the throne of Great Britain. It contains the constitutional provision that all future monarchs must join in communion with the Church of England, thus preventing Roman Catholics from becoming heirs to the British throne.

After the death of Queen Anne in 1714, the Elector of Hanover and Duke of Brunswick-Lünesborg was invited by the British Parliament to take the British throne. Although more than fifty Roman Catholics bore closer blood relationship to the British monarchy at that time, George had been Anne's closest living Protestant relative. George Louis of the German House of Hanover (who couldn't speak English and regarded himself as a German monarch on the British throne, as later did his son, George II) succeeded to the British crown as George I.

Therefore, during the eighteenth and nineteenth centuries, ties between Britain and Germany extended to a mutual Royal Family, the House of Hanover; a dynasty that would provide six monarchs after George I, who reigned until 1727. He was succeeded by George II (1727–60), George III (1760–1820), George IV (1820–30) and William IV (1830–37), who was then succeeded by Victoria. Queen Victoria reigned from 1837 to 1901. She was the daughter of the fourth son of King George III – whose successors had produced no legal heirs to the throne – and her German mother, Princess Victoria of Saxe-Coburg-Saalfeld.

Victoria's reign saw huge industrial expansion and the growth of a worldwide empire. Her marriage to her first cousin, the German Prince Albert of Saxe-Coburg-Gotha, created yet another German connection. Besides the enormous influence it had on British history, the House of Hanover also left a permanent mark on Britain's maps. Streets or terraces named 'Hanover', 'Brunswick', 'George', 'Frederick' or 'White Horse' are all likely to have been named in honour of Britain's German kings.

Victoria's husband Prince Albert (1819–1861) played a major role in the development of Great Britain during this period of history, although as Prince Consort he had no official power or duties. To the outside world Queen Victoria, Prince Albert, and their family seemed the embodiment of domestic bliss, but the historian Jane Ridley claims that the reality was very different.[1]

The marriage that took place on 10 February 1840 between the two first cousins – the young queen and the clever, handsome German prince – was a love match. Over seventeen years, nine children were born: four boys and five girls. Paintings and photographs projected an image of a virtuous, devoted young couple surrounded by obedient, fair-haired children.

Portrait of Queen
Victoria and Prince
Albert Consort.
(Hirarchivum Press /
Alamy Stock Photo).

Albert took over more and more of Victoria's work when her pregnancies forced her to step aside and Victoria admired him for his talents and ability, but deeply resented being robbed of her powers as queen; she also loathed being pregnant. This caused some terrible rows and it has been said that Albert was alarmed by Victoria's temper tantrums, fearing she might have inherited the madness of George III. While she stormed around the palace, he was reduced to putting notes under her door.

Originally unpopular with the British, Prince Albert soon won great respect for his strong sense of righteousness, his concern for the people, and his involvement in numerous public causes.[2] One of his main interests and greatest achievements was the improvement of the education system in Great Britain, which had not kept pace with the rapid industrial development of that time. His wide span of academic interests included all types of education, having experienced the need for adequate schooling for young children due to his and Victoria's large family of nine children. He actively supported the Educational Exhibition held in 1854 by the Royal Society of Arts, which provided a vital source of publicity for every type of education, including 'Friedrich Froebel's Kindergarten Ideology'. This revolutionised early childhood education for small children.

Froebel's ideology was introduced to Britain in 1851. The teaching of working class 'babies' had been predominately 'good behaviour and submission to rule' as well as learning 'off by heart' from a very early age as though they were adults. Instead of this formal learning and treatment of small children, which he considered wholly unsuitable, Froebel regarded play as being of central importance in the development of children's individual abilities. He claimed that interest fostered through activity encouraged creativity and spontaneity of expression and regarded play as a crucial guide for the teacher. Towards the end of the nineteenth century, many German-born teachers had been trained in the Froebel system, which was becoming more widespread. Making kindergarten education available to working class children was also supported by school inspectors in an attempt to counter inappropriate and formal teaching on young children. The School Board for London created the post of Instructor in the Kindergarten Method. Training courses were established and it was recognised that every infant school should have at least one teacher trained in this method. By the end of the century kindergarten methods of teaching had expanded to older children in infant schools in the three 'R' subjects of reading, writing and arithmetic. Whether the practice was entirely in accordance with Froebel's vision, having succumbed to a rigidity of interpretation, it is unquestionable that young children's experience of the educational process in English schools had been well and truly transformed.[3]

Prince Albert also saw the need for the modernisation of the university curriculum, public schools and the introduction of a wider education system for the working classes. In 1789, at the outbreak of the French Revolution, there had been 120 universities in Europe, including German universities, which numbered twenty-four, but only two universities in England. England's universities, Oxford and Cambridge, had been founded in the Middle Ages and academic interests, cloisters and relics of medievalism were in no way compatible with the technical requirements of a rapidly growing industrial nation. When Prince Albert was elected Chancellor of Cambridge University in 1847, achievements in the mathematical tripos and accomplishments in classics were supplemented with examinations in moral sciences including philosophy, history and law, as well as natural sciences.[4]

The modernisation of an inadequate curriculum in public schools as well as providing attainable education for working class children was also attained through his support. An example of this we can see in the development of Dulwich College, which is still a boarding and day independent school for boys in Dulwich, south-east London, founded in 1619 as a charitable school. During the mid-nineteenth century, it was badly in need of reform. When Prince Albert appointed the Rev. William Rogers, who had been a vicar in deprived London parishes, to the board of governors, an 'organised scheme of middle-class education for the children of clerks and tradesmen' was introduced with a wider syllabus. This school system, parallel to the development of Dulwich College, became widespread in schools around the area of London and later throughout the country, teaching more relevant subjects such as modern languages, science and physics, maths, literature, politics and the fine arts.

In 1845 Queen Victoria and Prince Albert visited Schloss Brühl on the Rhine as a guest of the Prussian court. During the visit, Prince Albert was impressed by efforts to improve chemical instruction on Prussian universities and equally impressed with the work of August Wilhelm Hofmann – one of a group of scientists eager to improve chemical instruction at the Prussian universities. Equally eager to improve chemical instruction in Britain, Prince Albert invited the young chemist to come and work in London with the promise of a much higher salary than he was already earning. As a result, Great Britain secured the services of August Wilhelm Hofmann, who achieved excellent results in the modernisation of academic chemistry. He also forged links among chemists and set the stage for the advancement of industrial chemistry in Britain.[5]

Prince Albert was intent upon securing the very best scientists for his adopted country. In the summer of 1855, the German chemist Justus von Liebig (1803–1873), born in Darmstadt (then in the Grand Duchy of Hesse) and widely credited as one of the founders of agricultural chemistry, received an invitation to spend the day with the British royal family at Osborne Castle. During the visit, he spent nearly three hours surveying the estate with the prince consort and learnt that the estate manager had followed much of his teachings on agriculture and chemistry based upon the analysis of organic compounds and the use of inorganic fertilizers on crops. Liebig's aim was to prevent famine and solve the problems of crop failure – as in Ireland and parts of Germany – through organic chemistry.

Personal friendships, public science and private enterprise shaped relationships as in the case of Liebig, who offered an intensive teaching and research programme on nitrogen-based fertilizers at his laboratory in Giessen, which also included British students. To signify close connections between British and German scientists, Liebig visited calico plants, paper mills, bleach works, potteries, breweries and other industries in Britain, urging his friends to 'unite their efforts with those of the chemists on the Continent.'

In his theory of nutrition, Liebig also stressed the importance of retaining nutritious cooking liquids after boiling meat. Seeing this as an inexpensive nutrition source for Europe's poor, he developed a formula for producing beef extract.

In 1865 together with the Belgian engineer George Christian Giebert, he founded Liebig's Extract of Meat Company, located in Fray Bentos, Uruguay, where cheap meat was available, and later trademarked the Oxo-brand beef bouillon cube. Liebig also promoted the use of baking powder to make lighter bread, studied the chemistry of coffee making, developed a breast milk substitute for babies who could not suckle, and has been claimed responsible for the development of Marmite.[6]

As President of the RSA – or the Royal Society for the Encouragement of Arts, Manufactures and Commerce – Prince Albert became heavily involved in the Great Exhibition of 1851. His active support for this massive show of new inventions and other technologies was partly due to his fascination for everything new. Through her husband, Queen Victoria also became interested in technological advances, which would make life easier for workers.

Organised with the help of Henry Cole (the inventor of the Christmas card), the Great Exhibition opened its doors on 1 May 1851 and came to end on 15 October 1851. It was held in London's Hyde Park, covering an area of 7.5 hectares, in a massive purpose-built structure of iron and thousands of panes of glass known as the Crystal Palace (The Crystal Palace was destroyed by fire in 1936) to promote the best of the British Empire. In the centre of this magnificent glass building stood an impressive 27-foot-high fountain constructed from pink glass.

The official illustrated catalogue listed exhibitors not only from throughout Britain and its 'Colonies and Dependencies', but also 'Forty-Four Foreign States' in Europe and the Americas. Over 100,000 objects were on display – half of these being from Britain. Six million people, including such famous Victorians as Charles Darwin, Samuel Colt, Charles Dickens, Emily Bronte, George Eliot and Lewis Carroll, together with around 12,000 German businessmen, industrialists and engineers, were impressed by the massive hydraulic press (designed by Stevenson), a steam hammer, counting machines, carpets, ribbons, printing machines, musical instruments, carriages, early versions of bicycles, agricultural machines, guns and watches.

The renowned Jacquard Loom, now in the Science Museum in London, was another great attraction; a power loom that could base its weave (and hence the design on the fabric) upon a pattern automatically read from punched wooden cards, held together in a long row by rope. Jacquard's technology was a real boon to mill owners, although it made many loom

The Crystal Palace from the north-east – Dickinson Brothers' collection of comprehensive pictures of the Great Exhibition of 1851. (Leonard Raven-Hill).

operators redundant. The exhibition also featured the first public toilet cubicles. The inventor of these, George Jennings, charged a penny – from which the expression 'spend a penny' originates. The Great Exhibition was a massive success and the money it raised was used to set up the Natural History Museum, the Science Museum and the Victoria & Albert Museum.

Financed by a profit of over £180,000 from the Great Exhibition, Prince Albert organised the purchase of a large swath of West London on which he built 'An Area of Culture and Learning'. This suburban estate in South Kensington was fondly known as 'Albertopolis' and a memorial statue of Prince Albert is located in front of the Royal Albert Hall. Some of the institutions in and around Albertopolis include: The Imperial College of London; Natural History Museum; The Royal Albert Hall; The Royal College of Art; The Royal College of Music; The Royal Geographical Society; The Royal Institute of Navigation; The Science Museum.[7]

When Prince Albert died in 1861, he had undoubtedly made remarkable achievements in many other fields besides education. One of these was his support for the abolition of slavery; another was his concern for factory workers. He visited countless factories, mines and other places of work and drew up plans for improving working conditions and housing. He occasionally intervened in political issues and, shortly before his death, used his influence to avert a possible war between Britain and the USA as a result of a dispute involving ships of the British and American navies during the American Civil War.

But despite the enthusiasm for innovative science, British leaders failed to import the whole of the German system of chemical instruction and application. The recently founded Royal College of Chemistry was financed through private subscriptions and private interests, which dominated the agenda and often neglected the German-style curriculum. By 1870 the German practise of visiting British farms had slowed down considerably and, after the death of Prince Albert in 1861, many scientists returned to Germany. Therefore, it was not long before the balance of ideas in agricultural chemistry, university training and research laboratories were able to overtake Britain in the chemical industry.[8]

8

Hostility Towards Germans

Throughout the centuries, latent hostility has existed in Britain towards foreigners considered to be over-represented in specific trades and industries, as well as political and social groupings. Early examples can be observed in the fifteenth century, when conflicts developed between Britain and the Hanseatic Merchants (Hanse) that continued well into the sixteenth century. At that time, the 'Steelyard' had become the largest medieval trading complex in Britain and had already extended its reach into Britain's cloth-making industry. It was not only English wool, but finished cloth which the Hansa exported, having finally gained control of the highly profitable cloth-making centres in Britain. In 1598 direct competition with British merchants was the cause of constant friction that ended in acts of violence. This induced Queen Elizabeth I to cut their privileges without dissolving the Hanseatic League entirely, which maintained a reliable source of communication between both countries during times of trouble, especially during the European blockade of the Napoleonic wars.[1]

From the mid-nineteenth century onwards, the British began to regard Germany as a threat. By the change of the century, the image of the German immigrant had undertaken a drastic change and signs of Germanophobia were becoming evident. One of the main reasons for such animosity was that Germans were willing to work for lower wages than their British counterparts, which resulted in unemployment among British workers.

Negative feelings towards Prince Albert, Queen Victoria's husband, which focused upon his German birth, remained latent until the 1850s. He was suspected of having played a leading role in the Prime Minister – Lord Russell's – dismissal of Lord Palmerston as Foreign Secretary. One journalist described the prince consort as being the chief agent of an 'Austro-Belgian-Coburg-Orleans clique, the avowed enemies of England'. Further hostility was expressed in a pamphlet which accused him of siding with Russia, Austria and Prussia, but this soon died down when sections of the press came to his defence.[2]

During the eighteenth and nineteenth centuries it was claimed that poor and destitute migrants were costing the government money that was needed elsewhere. Accusations of a lack of religious adherence among the German community in the east of London were made by the *London City Mission* magazine (perhaps an attempt to justify their own existence), followed by articles describing disgraceful conduct, drunkenness and vice that brought about hostile demonstrations against Germans in general. This developed into more latent economic hostility, which would later spread throughout British society.

Hostility towards German street bands grew between 1860 and the mid-1890s, focusing on their numbers and the noise they made, claiming that street musicians were a nuisance. They were often reduced to being called 'street beggars' and were the butt of negative comment in the press. They were also accused of being a hazard to London traffic because they frightened the horses. Noted persons including certain Members of Parliament complained of being disturbed in their concentration; of being interrupted in their work; or 'robbed of their time'. Four German brass band musicians were summoned before the magistrate on a charge of 'annoying people with their noise'. Newspaper articles described them as 'filthy German pigs who blackmailed householders by refusing to move until they had received a payment'.[3] This resulted in the introduction of a bill in Parliament for the suppression of street music whereby some members were of the opinion that many German bands were of great merit, pointing out that they often attracted large crowds and were 'well worth listening to'.

Hostility towards German waiters also became widespread during the late Victorian and Edwardian years. An article published in a prominent British trade magazine pointed out that English hotels were deluged with foreign workers and could 'quite understand the grievance of the English Hotel and Restaurant Union'.[4] By the end of the nineteenth century, a large number of hotels and restaurants throughout the country were already owned and run by Germans who preferred to employ their own countrymen, considering them to be more diligent workers than Britons. Before 1914 Germans would labour up to fifteen hours per day and relied upon tips, from which they could make £2 per week; this was in contrast to English waiters, who demanded a fixed wage. Germans also had formal training, which accounted for their 'neatness and civility'. A tongue-in-cheek article in the *Glasgow Herald* from 11 June 1907 gives a stereotype description of German waiters in Great Britain.

> The German waiter is the best in the world. He says so himself, and it is the truth … He is content with five hours sleep out of the twenty-four, and he always presents himself fresh and smiling … It is needless to say that in the majority of cases he is the superior in education and knowledge of the world of those whom he serves … With the German's natural aptitude for languages he has managed to make himself more or less proficient in the tongues of the various countries he has visited. This knowledge is invaluable to him, and he has little difficulty in getting a place in a hotel, restaurant, or café … He moves from place to place and from country to country, following money as the swallow follows summer. As a rule, the *kellner* has a high regard for Britain, but … as head waiter he does not get on very well with his British colleagues.

This led to the formation of the Loyal British Waiters Society in 1910 with 1,625 members at its inception. British people were requested to 'patronize and support' the interests of British waiters and a School of Instruction was established to improve the employment prospects of British waiters on realising that immigrants had received a full training.[5]

It was generally accepted that the improved education system in Germany was the reason for the success of German clerks in finding a niche in the British labour market.[6] Strong hostility in a speech of W. Field, MP for Dublin, claimed that, in 1902, 14,000 German clerks worked in Manchester, while the figure for London totalled an astronomical hundreds of thousands.[7] Stronger language was used in an article in the *National Review* of March 1910:

> German clerks act as "spies in the service of the enemy". Not only are our methods of business studied and sometimes improved upon, but the reports furnished to

headquarters disclose every weakness in our armour and show where openings offer for the protected wedge of German commerce to enter.[8]

Social and economic hostility led to the passing of the Aliens Act of 1905, introduced to control the arrival of poverty stricken migrants, but by this time Germans had become only a minor target regarding social migration since Germany's industrial revolution was already achieving an economic miracle regarding growth in population, urbanisation, industrialisation, production and commerce. By the mid-nineteenth century, German industries in coal, iron, steel, chemicals and railways were developing rapidly so that, by the end of the century, Germany had become a great power with a fast-growing industrial base equal to that of Great Britain.[9] This had been the result of the German Unification, which had taken place on the 18 January 1871 in the Versailles Palace in France after the previous confederation had been dissolved.

Wilhelm I of Prussia was beseeched to accept the title of Emperor of Germany – a politically and administratively integrated national state consisting of twenty-seven individually ruled territories. Otto von Bismarck became the first German Chancellor. The newly created German Empire replaced the Prussian Customs Union and managed to reduce competition between the existing twenty-seven constitutional territories as well as simplifying the export of goods.[10]

Wilhelm I was succeeded as Emperor of Germany by his son Prince Frederick William of Prussia, the future Frederick III, who died shortly after becoming Emperor (Kaiser), to be succeeded by his son, Wilhelm II.

Wilhelm II became Kaiser of Germany in 1888. His mother, Victoria, Princess Royal, was the eldest daughter of Queen Victoria and Prince Albert. She had married Prince Frederick William of Prussia. Historians have described Wilhelm II complex personality as intelligent, sometimes brilliant, with a taste for technology, industry and science. On the other hand, he was known to be superficial, impatient, arrogant and theatrical, with an exaggerated self-confidence and desire to show off. As a child, existing letters written

Portrait of Kaiser Wilhelm II in 1910; Bain News Service.

by his mother to his grandmother, Queen Victoria, describe the dominant interference in his upbringing by his German grandfather, Kaiser Wilhelm I, whom she blames for the difficult relationship with her problematic, weak child. Wilhelm II suffered from a withered right arm – a congenital infirmity for which he underwent excruciatingly painful but useless treatment during childhood. Determined to overcome this infirmity in his adult years, Wilhelm became an excellent horseman and sailor; he also spoke and dressed in a military manner. His distinct preference for wearing uniforms, which he changed numerous times during the day, suggests that he fancied himself as the supreme warlord. He was Queen Victoria's eldest grandchild and claimed himself to have been her favourite.

In 1890 William launched a 'New Course' in foreign affairs. True to his characteristic impatience, he refused to concede with the politics of an elder statesmen. In 1890 he dismissed the Chancellor, Otto von Bismarck – known as the 'Iron Chancellor' – who had been a dominant figure in the foundation of the German Empire after the repossession of German territories from France. Although William lacked the diplomatic finesse of a statesman, he was determined to encourage economic growth, and was largely successful. He succeeded in implementing 'personal rule' and, instead of allowing himself to be guided by experienced politicians, he refused to cooperate with Bismarck's successors and engaged politically unqualified civil servants as his advisers.

Wilhelm's craving for acceptance by his British relatives grew with his admiration for the Royal Navy. Despite being accepted by Queen Victoria as her favourite grandchild and being related to almost all the European royal houses, his relationship with British royalty, who found him arrogant and obnoxious, proved problematic. He had an especially bad relationship with his Uncle Bertie, the Prince of Wales (later King Edward VII), who treated him not as Emperor of Germany, but merely as another nephew. Wilhelm referred to his uncle as 'the old peacock' and, being an accomplished sailor, took impish delight in competing against his uncle in the yacht races at the annual Cowes Week on the Isle of Wight.[11]

Britain's confidence began to falter when German economic expansion showed signs of inducing a drastic change in the political landscape. Britain was gradually being squeezed out of European markets and becoming increasingly dependent on her empire, to which more and more of her exports went. Also, the rapid growth of Germany's expanding merchant fleet, which William had been determined should exceed the British, began to challenge even colonial markets. Good quality German products were the result of an excellent free education and training system that had already surpassed the British system in science, technical training and public welfare.

At the beginning of the twentieth century Wilhelm began to build the German navy, intending that Germany should be declared a world power. Being a prolific ship builder and draftsman, he spent hours drawing sketches of the ships he wanted built, leaving his chancellor to look after domestic affairs. Because his increasingly eccentric views on foreign affairs were spreading further alarm throughout Europe, defence alliances were formed between Britain, Japan, France and Russia, even though the German government failed to understand why strained relationships had developed with Britain.

It was feared that the Germans would soon be invading Great Britain. A whole series of novels and short stories gave realistic descriptions of invasions by the 'Huns', which people read and believed to be actually taking place. In 1906, a novel called *The Invasion of 1910* was written by William Le Queux – one of the leading authors of invasion literature. Viewed as a prime example of pre-First World War Germanophobia, it preached the need to prepare for war with Germany.[12] Similar types of literature described Germans as being uncouth and arrogant, stressing barbarism, dullness and drunkenness despite touristic admiration of the Rhine and the German landscape in general. Journalists published critical reports and political speeches denouncing Germany's expansionist policy. After the press baron Lord Northcliffe visited Germany in 1909, an article in the *Daily Mail* described a country of 'business and battleships'. Fears were reinforced by the Kaiser's unguarded remarks about 'becoming the Admiral of the Atlantic', suggesting 'we can ride down our enemies'; remarks that were regarded as threats to the British. Passionate speeches depicted war against a background of widespread xenophobia and scaremongering; rumours that Germans in Britain were spies waiting to be activated as soon the invasion began resulted in mass hysteria and widespread hatred against Germans, as well as anything remotely connected with Germany. This also included the strict avoidance of goods 'made in Germany'. To avoid further discrimination, many business owners and wealthier Germans became British nationals and anglicised their names. Even the Royal family thought it prudent to change 'Saxe-Coburg-Gotha' to 'Windsor'.

Yet there were still extensive commercial links between the two countries as well as mutual assistance in business enterprises; not everyone believed that Germany would, or even could, invade Britain. Organisations were founded with the intention of improving relations since hostility had not yet saturated the British society as it would during later years. German businesses still flourished in Great Britain; German pork butcher's shops could be found in almost every town; hotels and restaurants employed German personal and served British customers with German beer; scientists, teachers, manufacturers, merchants and office workers were among the 53,324 Germans recorded in major areas of settlement by the census statistics of 1911, without taking into account second and third generations who had since become British nationals.

In 1908 Kaiser Wilhelm, already noted for his fiery and chauvinistic rhetoric, his excitable character and theatrical behaviour, made a damaging personal blunder that cost him much prestige among his subjects. This blunder has become known as the '*Daily Telegraph* Affair', which originated from an interview with Wilhelm and was published in 1908. Instead of promoting his ideas on an Anglo-German friendship that, according to one of his advisors, had been his intention, a sudden and emotional outburst during the course of the interview produced wild statements and diplomatically damaging remarks. He ended up by further alienating not only the British, but also the French, Russians, and Japanese, implying among other things that the Germans cared nothing for the British. He continued to make damaging statements about the French and Russians in connection with the Second Boer War and claimed that the German naval build-up was targeted against the Japanese and not Britain. Finally, he rounded off his verbal rampage by blustering; 'You English are mad, mad, mad as March hares.'

The effect of this blunder in Germany was significant; there were serious calls for his abdication, which induced him to keep a low profile for months after this fiasco and seriously impaired his self-confidence. Soon afterwards he suffered from a severe bout of depression, from which he never fully recovered, and he lost much of the influence he had previously exercised in domestic and foreign policy.

At the beginning of the twentieth century, a complicated alliance system prevalent in Europe in the form of numerous treaties interconnecting various states brought about a precarious political situation in Europe. William's attitude towards the growing conflict was both erratic and ambivalent. At first he appeared unwilling to accept the opinions of his military advisors and changed his mind from one minute to the next as to whether war should be declared or not. Unable to make up his mind, and obviously confused as to the unexpected turn of events for the worse, he failed to control his generals who believed that Germany's interests would be best served by war, and as soon as possible.[13]

9

THE EFFECTS OF WAR

The onset of the First World War cannot be blamed on Germany as a whole; also, the commonly held notion that the war started out of outrage over the assassination of Archduke Franz Ferdinand of Austria and his wife Sophie at the hands of Serbian nationalists is not entirely correct. Austria's Emperor Franz Josef was said to have been relieved to be rid of an heir he disliked and most people agreed it had been for the best. Austria-Hungary had been looking for an excuse to wage a preventative war against Serbia in order to regain territory they had lost during the Balkan Wars; this territory had given them access to the Adriatic Sea. They had not taken it back previously, having lacked German support and fearing trouble with Russia who had a defence treaty with Serbia.

With the assassination of Archduke Franz Ferdinand and his wife on 28 June 1914, Austria-Hungary was able to secure German support after William had consulted his cousins Tsar Nicholas II, who privately confirmed that he had no intention of going to war over the treaty with Serbia. Now with Germany's support and believing that Russia had no intention of entering the fray, Austria-Hungary issued a severe ultimatum to Serbia that they felt sure would be rejected, providing them with the opportunity to declare war. Surprisingly, Serbia's response towards the ultimatum was mostly positive with the exception of a few minor details. This, however, gave Austria-Hungary the excuse to declare war against Serbia. At this point, existing treaties between European countries began to take effect.

Tsar Nicholas ignored his agreement with Wilhelm and decided to come to Serbia's aid.

France, being bound by a treaty with Russia, was now at war with Germany by association.

Germany then decided to invade Belgium, having received 'absolutely unimpeachable information' that the French planned to attack the German army via Belgium.

Although Britain had informed Wilhelm that they intended to remain neutral, they were suddenly reminded of a seventy-five-year-old defence agreement with Belgium and declared war against Germany on 4 August 1914, after Germany had refused to withdraw from Belgium.

Because Britain was now at war with Germany, so were their colonies; Canada, India, Australia, New Zealand and South Africa were also compelled to enter the war. Furthermore, Japan, who had an existing treaty with Britain, declared war on Germany; Austria-Hungary then declared war on Japan for declaring war on Germany.

Therefore, a minor territorial skirmish developed into the First World War, what has been described as 'the war to end all wars' because of the unparalleled scale of death and devastation it caused.[1]

The war had also a ruinous effect on the German population of Great Britain when news of German atrocities in Belgian hit the headlines; large-scale massacres, rape and pillaging soldiers who left a trail of burned towns and villages behind them. Another wave of hatred exploded with the sinking of the RMS *Lusitania*, regarded as the second most famous ship to be lost at sea after the *Titanic*. This was a major event of the war, which on 6 April 1917 led to the Americans joining its allies, Britain, France and Russia, to fight in the First World War.

Much has been written about the sinking of the *Lusitania* on Friday 7 May 1915, off the coast of Ireland, when the German submarine *U-20* fired a torpedo into her hull. *Lusitania* sank within eighteen minutes and the loss of life was of a terrible scale; 1,198 people died – 785 passengers and 413 crew. Questions related to the sinking on its route from New York to Liverpool have never been satisfactorily answered. What cannot be denied is the fact that when transatlantic passengers were routinely required to check departure times in the press, they were surprised to find a second notice alongside the ship's sailing times. This had been posted by the German government warning them that they were about to sail into a war zone and that this carried great risk. More than two months had passed since Germany had declared that allied ships caught in British waters would be sunk without warning, but influential Americans (of German extraction) cautioned that such callousness could not be applied to a passenger liner without recrimination.

On 7 May 1915 passengers and crew on board the *Lusitania* felt a dull thud followed by an ear-splitting explosion – or two. It was carrying a large amount of ordnance for the British army including 4.2 million bullets. In spite of a dispute as to whether this could be labelled as contraband, the British government exploited the sinking of the *Lusitania* as a propaganda gift and set up an enquiry into the disaster. The prominent legal figure who chaired the enquiry described the affair as 'a damned dirty business'. His report has never been published and no copies have yet been issued.[2]

Many of the ship's crew were from Liverpool; the majority from the close knit Irish community of Liverpool. Reports suggest that the first signs of trouble came from family and friends of the dead sailors when riots broke out across Liverpool. They spread not only throughout Britain but to other cities across the world. Such was the impact of *Lusitania*. In London and other larger cities with German communities, mobs attacked their properties and vandalised their shops, especially those of German butchers whose families lived above their shops and were easy victims of violence. When the sons of naturalised Germans serving in the British army were home on leave, to appease aggression they would often wear their uniforms while helping behind the counter. Also, many Germans anglicised their names.

Non-naturalized German males of military age found themselves behind the barbed wire of internment camps that had been opened throughout the country. Wives and children were deported back to Germany, often to a country they no longer knew and a language they no longer understood.

The largest internment camp was Knockaloe on the Isle of Man, which had taken on the size of a small town. By 1915 it reached a peak population of 24,000 men, including those unlucky German tourists or ship's passengers of military age who happened to be in British territory at the outbreak of war. Prisoners lived in wooden huts divided into sections holding thirty men, with provision for food and pastimes. Despite their longing for the outside world and the families they had left behind, prisoners participated in and developed a wide scope of activities such as gardening and growing vegetables. They formed theatre groups, clubs and societies. Barbers and bakers carried out their trades behind barbed wire because of the demand for their services and some even obtained

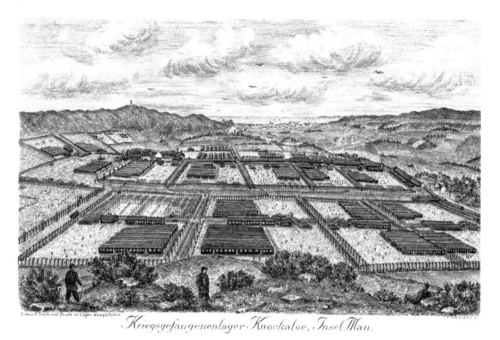

Kriegsgefangenenlager · Knockaloe, Insel Man.

The largest internment camp was Knockaloe on the Isle of Man.

paid work.[3] Although the Hague Convention forbade civilian detainees and prisoners of war from working, most of them were eager to earn money to support their families, or simply to combat monotony in camp life. By the end of 1915, MPs began asking questions in Parliament about the employment of both civilian and military internees and, as a result, by July 1916 between 3,000 and 4,000 enemy aliens 'were employed on work that was to the public advantage'.

Between 1917 and 1919 the employment of enemy aliens and prisoners of war had become a complex operation, despite the numerous rules and regulations of the Hague Convention as well as objections and protests from the German government. By early 1918 almost 2,000 German civilians were working outside internment camps throughout Great Britain, although they were not allowed to work with British civilians or where an adequate number of British workers were available. They received payment averaging about 1.5 pence per day and obtained higher food rations of 2,700 calories daily instead of the normal ration of 2,000 calories.[4] Agriculture was a significant area of employment and prisoners played an important role in securing the harvest. Most of them performed their jobs effectively, although some worked slowly due to limited experience and inadequate food supplies. Other occupations included forestry, land reclamation, building work, road and railway maintenance and construction, dock work, brick making, quarrying, brush making, aerodrome construction and various other employments.

Nevertheless, prisoners were still confronted with hostility and the all-encompassing Germanophobia that characterised Britain during the First World War, despite their vital contribution to war time food production, mining and general infrastructure. On the other hand, close and often life long friendships developed between farmers and their German farm hands. Animosity grew between steel workers in Port Talbot who threatened to go on strike if prisoners were employed in the construction of new steel works. Mine workers on the Scottish island of Raasay protested against the

Trade protectionist British Empire Union. An anti-German poster, from approximately 1919, calling for the boycott of German goods and depicting German business people selling their products in Britain as 'the other face' of German soldiers who committed atrocities during the First World War.

employment of prisoners during a strike and strong protests occurred 'against the employment of German prisoners in building operations at Chepstow while British trade union men were being discharged'.

Despite public animosity and protests from returned British soldiers who had not found employment, the number of working prisoners gradually increased. By 1919 it had peaked at 50,585 German workers, including 17,100 in agriculture. By the end of the war, 62,500 prisoners were employed including 26,000 agricultural workers, although by October 1919, as repatriation took place, numbers had reduced to around 3,000 workers.

The Treaty of Versailles blamed Germany for the First World War, therefore they had to suffer the consequences. It lost 25,000 square miles of its territory and 7 million subjects to France, Belgium, Czechoslovakia, Poland, Lithuania and Denmark. The League of Nations took over the Saarland district on the French border and Germany lost all of its colonial possessions; German South West Africa and German East Africa, German Samoa and territories in Asia were taken by the Allies. The German army was basically stripped and restricted to 100,000 men; they were not allowed aircraft, tanks or submarines, and any materials needed to create these objects were also restricted. The navy was not dismantled, but permitted to have only a limited number of battleships, cruisers and destroyers.

Kaiser Wilhelm was said to have been greatly shocked when the German civilian government and public opinion demanded his abdication. In late 1918 mutiny among the ranks of his beloved Kaiserliche Marine confirmed his decision to abdicate and on 10 November 1918 Wilhelm went into exile in the Netherlands, which had remained neutral throughout the war. Although Article 227 of the Treaty of Versailles had expressly provided for the prosecution of Wilhelm for a supreme offence against international morality and the sanctity of treaties, Queen Wilhelmina and the Dutch government refused to extradite him, despite appeals from the Allies. King George V wrote that he looked on his cousin as the greatest criminal in history, but opposed Prime Minister David Lloyd George's proposal to 'hang the Kaiser'. President Woodrow Wilson of the United States rejected extradition, arguing that punishing Wilhelm for waging war would destabilize international order and lose the peace. Wilhelm accepted the reality and purchased a country house in the municipality of Doorn in Holland, known as Huis Doorn. He moved in on 15 May 1920 and it remained his home for the remainder of his life until his death in 1941.

The Treaty of Versailles demanded that Germany pay reparation of $5 billion to the Allies for war damage – a sum Germany could never pay off within the next hundred years. The Allies, which were France, Britain and America, since the Russian Empire had collapsed during the revolution after the abdication of Tsar Nicholas II, insisted upon terms that Germany could not accept, considering the country was 'as poor as a church mouse and people were starving'.

There were doubts among British politicians as to whether Germany had been wholly responsible for the war.[5] In 1925 Gilbert Murray, who was chairman of the League of Nations Union, remarked that 'hardly any reasonable person in England continues to talk of Germany as solely responsible for the war'. It is therefore hardly surprising that the social breach from 1914 to 1918 between Britons and Germans was quickly healed, beginning with a meeting of trade unionists led by Ernest Bevin. In 1947, as Secretary of State for Foreign Affairs, Bevin was known to feel uncomfortable in the company of Germans. He is quoted as remarking to the British Military Governor in Germany, General Sir Brian Robertson – who enjoyed quoting this to others – 'I tries 'ard, Brian, but I 'ates 'em'.

After the First World War, William Le Queux's dated tales of German spies were no longer in demand and stopped making an impact upon British society. The League of Nations advocated normal relations between the two countries, which began with exchange visits between musical and dance groups. Despite growing sympathy from both sides, it was becoming more and more obvious that Germany's economical problems and disastrous shortage of food could only be solved by revising the Treaty of Versailles. However, this would not happen due to worsening relations between Britain and France, so that certain clauses of the agreement preventing economic growth were simply ignored.[6]

The Weimar Republic came into existence as a semi-presidential representative democracy on 11 August 1919, when a new constitution was written. During its fourteen years of existence, the Weimar Republic faced numerous problems including hyperinflation and social unrest, as well as political extremism and problematic relationships with the victors of the First World War. Alternatively, the Weimar Republic government successfully reformed currency, unified tax policies and organized the railway system, as well as eliminating most of the requirements of the Treaty of Versailles. Germany never completely fulfilled disarmament requirements, paid only a small portion of war reparations and continued to dispute the Eastern border.

More negative effects were caused by the Great Depression – a severe worldwide economic depression that originated in the United States. It was brought about by the sudden and missive fall in stock prices followed shortly after by the stock market crash on 29 October 1929 that became known as 'Black Tuesday'. The Great Depression had a devastating global effect among rich and poor that lasted until the beginning of the Second World War.

Yet, before 1933, an enthusiastically positive image of Germany had developed. Foreign visitors enjoyed the free, exciting, and modern image of Berlin's 'golden twenties', which gave no inclination of the forthcoming disaster. In 1933 Adolf Hitler became the new German Chancellor of a coalition government, which eventually wiped out constitutional governance and civil liberties. With Hitler's seizure of power, Germany's first tentative democracy collapsed. A single-party state heralded the beginning of the Nazi era – and Germany's descent into barbarism.

Germany's Loss, Britain's Gain

The most significant arrivals in twentieth-century Britain were German Jewish refugees, forced from their homes by Nazi persecution. Between 1933 and 1945, around 59,000 German nationals were given asylum in Britain. Some moved on to America, others returned to Germany after the war, but many settled in Britain. Academics began to arrive in Britain when Nazi legislation began forcing universities to sack all Jews, however distinguished. Germany's loss was Britain's gain. This group of German scholars-in-exile produced over sixteen Nobel Laureates, seventy Fellows of the Royal Society and thirty-five Fellows of the British Academy.

Erich Mendelsohn was a Jewish German architect born 1887 in Allenstein, East Prussia. He studied architecture at the Technical University of Berlin, was later known for his expressionist and futuristic architecture, and became one of the most influential architects of the twentieth century. In 1933, the Nazis seized his considerable fortune, struck his name from the German Architects' Union, and excluded him from the Prussian Academy of Arts. Mendelsohn fled to England and began a successful but short partnership with Serge Chermayeff.

In 1935 they designed the famous De La Warr Pavilion, a Grade One listed building on the seafront at Bexhill on Sea on the south coast of England, which is often claimed to be the first modernist public building in Britain.

Nikolaus Pevsner (1902–1983) was a German/Jewish, later British, scholar of historical architecture. He taught at the University of Göttingen from 1929 to 1933, offering a specialist course on English art and architecture, but was forced to resign due to Nazi race laws. After moving to England he was given a research fellowship at Birmingham University, but during the Second World War spent three months internment in Liverpool as an enemy alien. After the war he published numerous books on contemporary design and modern architecture.

> A bicycle shed is a building; Lincoln Cathedral is a piece of architecture. Nearly everything that encloses space on a scale sufficient for a human being to move in is a building; the term architecture applies only to buildings designed with a view to aesthetic appeal. [7]

Pevsner also described the three ways aesthetic appeal could manifest itself in architecture as being in a building's façade, the material volumes, or the interior.

Apart from his career as a writer, editor and broadcaster, Pevsner lectured architectural history at Cambridge for almost thirty years and held the Slade Professorship of Fine Art for a record six years from 1949 to 1955. He also held the Slade professorship at Oxford in 1968. Having assumed British citizenship in 1946, Pevsner was awarded a CBE in 1953 and was knighted in 1969 'for services to art and architecture'. Sir Nikolaus Bernhard Leon Pevsner died in London in 1983.

Another famous pioneer of modernist architecture and design was Walter Gropius (1883–1969). He was the founder of the world-famous Bauhaus School and Faculty in Dessau, which specialised in well-designed industrially produced objects. Despite the fact that he had served in the First World War and been awarded the Iron Cross for bravery, the rise of Hitler in the 1930s drove Gropius out of Germany. He lived and worked in Britain before moving to America in 1937, where he continued his career as an outstanding architect and designer of several award-winning buildings.

The Nazi accession to power had also affected musicians from every corner of German society, and numerous well-known Jewish composers, conductors, musicologists, instrumentalists and singers suffered through repressive actions and legislation.

Fritz Busch (1890–1951), who originated from a German family of famous musicians, was a renowned conductor and pianist. Although he was not himself Jewish, he counted many Jews among his friends and was opposed to Nazi dictatorship. He had already worked at several opera houses before being appointed musical director of the Dresden State Opera in 1922. During his tenure of eleven years he kept the opera at the highest level and premiered works by Richard Strauss, Ferruccio Busoni and Kurt Weill among others. Five weeks after Hitler came to power in 1933, Busch was publically removed from his post at the Dresden State Opera in a politically motivated and humiliating dismissal. In 1934, together with Carl Ebert, a fellow musician who had fled from the Nazis, he became the music director of Glyndebourne Festival Opera in England where he remained until the outbreak of the Second World War in 1939, and to which he later returned in 1950. His brothers were the distinguished violinist Adolf Busch and the cellist Hermann Busch. His son, Hans Busch, later became stage director at the Indiana University Opera. Fritz Busch died in London in 1951.

The Amadeus Quartet consisted of four musicians with exceptional qualities. Norbert Brainin, the first violin, Siegmund Nissel and Peter Schidlof were all Jewish refugees from Vienna who first met in internment camps in Britain in 1940. Martin Lovett, the cellist, joined them not long after the war, at a moment when the musical climate was sympathetic to chamber music and the record industry was booming. The (unofficial) debut of the 'Brainin Quartet' in 1947 was a huge success; the proper debut of the Amadeus Quartet on 10 April 1948 in London was a sensation; so too was its 1950 debut on German soil, in Hamburg, where 'the audience in its enthusiasm almost smashed the entire hall'.

Hans Keller was a highly talented violinist, born in 1919 into a wealthy and culturally well-connected Jewish family in Vienna. In 1938 he was forced to flee to London (where he had relatives), although he had been interned at Knockaloe on the Isle of Man as an enemy alien at the beginning of the First World War. Later he studied the violin and viola at the Royal Academy of Music and in the years that followed as an accomplished musician he became a popular music journalist and broadcaster with BBC.

Andrew Sachs was born in Berlin in 1930 as Andreas Siegfried Sachs. He left with his parents for Britain in 1938 when he was eight years old to escape the Nazis, his father being Jewish and his mother half Austrian. Later he made his name on British television and is best known for his portrayals of comical Spanish waiter Manuel in *Fawlty Towers* and Ramsay Clegg in *Coronation Street*.

But the refugees that caught the public imagination were the 10,000 unaccompanied Jewish children, brought to Britain through the Kindertransport rescue-mission. For the children, the relief of escaping was mixed with the pain of leaving parents behind, and the uncertain future ahead.

10

VICTORY AND DEFEAT

In 1945, Britain's power was unmatched by any other European state. Germany, at the other end of scale, was in a desperate situation, experiencing what has been called 'the zero hour'. Military defeated, physically ruined, economically bankrupt and morally and politically discredited, the country was at the mercy of its occupiers after unconditional surrender on 8 May 1945. It had lost its power, its unity and sovereignty as well as its national identity along with any trace of independent dignity. Prominent British politicians openly expressed their views that Germans were prone to militarism and aggression. A continuation of pre-war Germanophobia was kept alive, along with emerging details and press reports of appalling atrocities in German concentration camps; a genocide perpetrated by the Nazis that killed around 11 million people, the majority of whom were Jews. Three quarters of a century later, Germany's desire for reparation towards victims of the Nazi era is still of major significance.

After capitulation, the German people, like their leaders, were preoccupied with the normalisation of relations with those European neighbours who had suffered most during the Second World War and especially the Jews. Uppermost, they were having to come to terms with the fact that the vast majority of them, willingly or not, consciously or not, had supported a murderous regime by closing their eyes to its brutality.[1] They were also preoccupied with meeting the demands of three occupying powers – America, Russia and Great Britain – although the understanding of democracy, which had never been a stable factor in German history, varied enormously between West and East.

Allied powers were now concerned with governing and exploiting their individual territorial settlements, which involved determining what Germany had to offer its victors as a symbol of retribution. Pre-war policies in Britain had not been adequately concerned with the results of fifteen years of secret planning by the Nazi regime. In their bid to revolutionise warfare, the German military had conspired with scientists, engineers and industrialists to produce weapons that would render all previous tactics obsolete. The British way of thinking had remained on the battlefields of the First World War and had also remained amazingly indifferent to Germany's rearmament, which was finally revealed as an astonishing achievement with superb inventions in comparison to Britain's relationship with its industry regarding the development of modernised weapons, which had hardly existed in Britain. Despite reports that the German army would be ready for battle by 1939, British officials had remained sceptical, predicting that the German economy and industry would collapse within two years of war because of the blockade on essential minerals, chemicals and petroleum products. This, however, had proved to be a fateful miscalculation of Germany's ability to produce a whole range of substitutes that neutralised the Allied blockade and heralded the dawn of a new scientific era.[2]

During the course of the war, which was declared on 3 September 1939, both American and British Army chiefs privately acknowledged that their soldiers were fighting with inferior weapons.[3] After the war, Allied investigators established that the very survival of the isolated Third Reich during four years of war can be attributed to their technical superiority.

Four months after Germany's defeat, the British industry – exhausted, inflexible and inefficient – was traumatically grappling with the problems of converting to peacetime production[4] until a handful of enlightened industrialists and officials acknowledged the importance of German expertise for Britain's recovery. It was argued that 'German refugees had helped Britain considerably during the war and other Germans could help over the long term now'. In truth, a solution was urgently needed for Britain's huge debts; unemployment was rising steeply and hopes of trade recovery had dimmed.

An astonishing battle began between the Allies in the aftermath of war to seize the spoils of Nazi Germany and to plunder German technology in part-exchange for enormous war compensation debts. This became known as the 'Paperclip Conspiracy'. Due to the ferocious American and Russian recruitment of German scientists and engineers, the British government finally agreed that the alternative solution was to bring – or hijack – a maximum of 200 German key-scientists and technicians to Britain and settle them down in British industry. In 1944, while the Russians were preoccupied with the dismantling of German production factories in the Russian zone and transporting them lock, stock and barrel back to Russia, a colossal search was set in motion by British Intelligence for war secrets in occupied German territory before they were destroyed or fell into Soviet hands.

Declassified government documents discovered decades later by the journalist and author Ian Cobain in the National Archives at Kew, have revealed extensive details of the secret programme to hijack Germany's scientific and technological trade secrets to Great Britain. An elite British Army unit known as T-Force captured and abducted hundreds of German scientists and technicians and put them to work at government ministries and private firms in the UK in an attempt to boost British business and, as the Cold War developed, to prevent the Soviet Union from benefiting from Nazi scientific and industrial assets. A memo written by a civil servant working with the British military in Germany in 1946 explained the procedure:

> Usually an NCO arrives without notice at the house or office of the German and warns that he will be required. He does not give him any details of the reasons, nor does he present his credentials. Sometime later the German is seized (often in the middle of the night) and removed under guard.

Abductions were carried out in the British-controlled zone of post-war Germany by an organisation called the 'British Intelligence Objectives Sub-Committee', or 'Bios'. German businessmen were forced to travel to Britain for questioning by their commercial rivals with threats of internment should they refuse to reveal trade secrets. After interrogation, which could last for months, they were either released or put to work in Britain for a wage of 15s per week. Documents give information as to the round-up (or enforced evacuation to Great Britain) of fifty scientists in 1945, with many complaining over the loss of their homes, jobs and pensions. Initially, no provision had been made for wives and children left behind in Germany, who hardly had a roof over their heads. The most devastating bombing had struck the residential areas at the heart of the cities;

hunger was the predominant problem among civilians, especially women with children who had escaped the bombing. Many had fled in terror from the torture and raping of the oncoming Russian army on their way from east to west during the final months of the war.

In many cases Germans were unwilling to surrender scientific data and special units were formed by British and American Allies to interrogate scientists and technicians as well as unearth files kept in hiding places; for example a cache in a warehouse wall of an optical company in Wetzlar near Frankfurt revealed secret files on optical instruments, microscopy, and aiming devices. The German Patent Office had put some of its most secret patents down a 1,600-foot mine shaft at Heringen in Hessen, beneath a pile of liquid-oxygen cylinders. When Joint Intelligence Objectives teams found them, it was doubtful that they could be saved. They were legible, but in such bad shape that a trip to the surface would cause them to disintegrate. Photo equipment and a crew were therefore lowered into the shaft and a complete microfilm record was made of the patents there.

Among the shattered rubble of a nation, investigators searched for machinery, research papers and patents that could be shipped back to Britain. The mass of documents was mountainous. Later it was reported that tens of thousands of tons of material were involved, estimated at over a million separate items likely to contain practically all the scientific, industrial and military secrets of Nazi Germany. It has been called 'the greatest single source of this type of material in the world, and the first orderly exploitation of an entire country's brainpower divided between the four Allied powers'.[5]

British industrialists were eager to learn as much as they could from the Germans, from the mining of coal to the making of perfume. According to the National Archives, companies that employed German scientists and technicians immediately after the Second World War included:

- ICI, the chemicals giant.
- Courtaulds, the manufacturer of fabric, clothing, and artificial fibres.
- Pears, the soap and cosmetics company.
- Yardley, the maker of fragrances and toiletries.
- Coal Oil Development, a company based in Swansea.
- BSA Tools, the Birmingham machine toolmaker.

An English manufacturer would name his German counterpart and competitor and 'invite' him to England (whether the man came voluntarily or not is questionable). They would then discuss business and the German would be gently persuaded to reveal secrets of his trade. In case he refused, he would be kept in polite internment until he became tired of not being allowed to return to his family, and then he would tell the Englishman what he wanted to know. Thus, for about £6 per day, the English businessman would gain Germany's economic secrets. What else did they find? Here are some outstanding samples from the war secrets collection:

- The secret production method of the tiniest vacuum tube, which was about half the size of a thumb and made from heavy porcelain instead of glass, making it virtually indestructible.
- A magnetophone tape made from plastic strips and metallised on one side with iron oxide. In Germany it had been invented for phonograph recordings and was a forbearer of today's recording tape.
- An infrared device with a remarkably small generator had been invented for seeing at night, thus enabling German vehicles to see objects clearly within a distance of

200 metres and army tanks to spot targets 2 miles away. As a sniper scope it enabled German riflemen to pick off a man in total blackness. The small generator, 5 inches across, stepped up voltage from an ordinary flashlight battery to 15,000 volts! It had a walnut-sized motor that spun a rotor at 10,000 rpm – so fast that originally it had destroyed all lubricants with the great amount of ozone it produced. The Germans developed a new type of grease – chlorinated paraffin oil – that enabled the generator to run 3,000 hours.

- The technique and the machine for making the world's most remarkable electric capacitor also fell into Allied hands. Millions of capacitors had been essential to the radio and radar industry. Previous capacitors had always been made of metal foil; this one was made of paper, coated with 1/250,000 of an inch of vaporized zinc as well as being 40 per cent smaller and 20 per cent cheaper than other capacitors. In case of a fuse or breakdown, the zinc film evaporated, the paper immediately insulated, and the capacitor was right again. It kept on working through multiple breakdowns, at 50 per cent higher voltage than previous capacitors.
- In textiles the war secrets collection produced many revelations. A German rayon-weaving machine was found to increase production in relation to floor space by 150 per cent. A 'Links to Links' loom produced ladder-resistant, run-proof hosiery. It has been claimed that new German needle-making machinery revolutionised that trade in both the United Kingdom and the United States. Another discovery was a method of putting a crimp in viscose rayon fibres giving them the appearance of warmth and resistance to wear, as well as altering its reaction to wool dyes. Investigators discovered that the secret here was the addition to the cellulose of 25 per cent fish protein.

But of all the industrial secrets, perhaps the biggest windfall came from the laboratories and plants of the great German cartel I. G. Farben Industrie. Never before, it has been claimed, was there such a storehouse of secret information. It covered liquid and solid fuels, metallurgy, synthetic rubber, textiles, chemicals, plastics, drugs and dyes.

In matters of food, medicine, and branches of the military art, the discoveries of search teams were no less impressive; in aeronautics and guided missiles they proved downright alarming.

One of the food secrets the Nazis had discovered was a way to sterilize fruit juices without heat. The juice was filtered, then cooled, then carbonated and stored under eight atmospheres of carbon dioxide pressure. Later, the carbon dioxide was removed; the juice passed through another filter – which this time germ-proofed it – and then was bottled. Milk pasteurization by ultraviolet light had, until then, always failed in other countries, but the Germans had found how to do it by using light tubes of great length, simultaneously enriching milk with Vitamin-D.

At a plant in Kiel, British searchers of the Joint Intelligence Objectives Committee found that cheese was being produced using a newly discovered high-speed method. A good quality Hollander and Tilster could be made within eighty minutes – from the renneting to the hooping of the curd. Butter (in a creamery near Hamburg) was being produced by something long wished for by butter-makers all over the world – a continuous butter making machine. It was an invention of dairy equipment manufacturers in Stuttgart; taking up less space and turning out 1,500 pounds of butter in the hour. The machine was promptly shipped to be tested by the American Butter Institute.

Among other food innovations was a German way of making yeast in almost limitless quantities. The waste sulphite liquor from the beech wood used to manufacture cellulose was treated with an organism known to bacteriologists as candida arborea at temperatures higher than ever used in yeast manufacture before. The finished product served as both animal and human food. Its caloric value was four times that of lean meat, and contained twice as much protein.

The Germans had also developed new methods of preserving food by plastics and new, advanced refrigeration techniques. Refrigeration and air-conditioning on German U-boats had become so efficient that the submarines could travel from Germany to the Pacific, operate there for two months, and then return to Germany without having to take on fresh water for the crew. A secret plastic mixture (among its ingredients were polyvinyl acetate, chalk, and talc) was used to coat bread and cheese. A loaf fresh from the oven was dipped, dried, re-dipped, and then heated half an hour at 285 degrees, keeping it fresh and edible for eight months.

As for medical secrets, one Army surgeon remarked upon the years of research that would now be saved, referring to the German technique for treatment after prolonged and usually fatal exposure to cold. This discovery reversed everything medical science had thought about the subject. In every one of the dreaded experiments subjects were successfully revived, both temporarily and permanently, by immediate immersion in hot water. In two cases of coronary standstill and cessation of respiration, a hot bath at 122 degrees brought both subjects back to life, which is generally accepted by medicine today.

German medical researchers had discovered a way to produce synthetic blood plasma, which was named 'Capain', made on a commercial scale and equalled natural plasma in results. Another discovery was 'Periston' – a substitute for the blood liquid. An oxidation production of adrenalin (Adrenichrome) was produced in quantity successfully only by the Nazis and was used with good results in combating high blood pressure.

Likewise of great importance medically was research done by Dr Boris Fojewksky of the Kaiser Wilhelm Institute of Biophysics at Frankfurt in the ionization of air as related to health. Positively ionized air was discovered to have deleterious effects upon human well-being and accounted for the discomfort and depression felt at times when the barometer was falling. In many cases its presence brought on asthma, hay fever, nervous tension and raised high blood pressure to danger point. It would bring on the symptoms common in mountain sickness, such as laboured and rapid breathing, dizziness, fatigue and sleepiness. Dr Fojewksky discovered that negatively ionized air produced the opposite effect – it created a feeling of high spirits and well-being, and wiped out mental depression; it also steadied breathing, reduced high blood pressure and checked allergies and asthma.

But of highest significance for the future were the Nazi secrets in aviation and in various types of missiles. An Army Air Force publication reported that the V-2 rocket, which had bombed London, 'was just a toy compared to what the Germans had up their sleeve.'

When the war ended, 138 types of guided missiles were found to be in various stages of production or development, using every kind of remote control and fuse such as radio, radar, wire, continuous wave, acoustics, infrared, light beams and magnetics to name but a few. For power, all methods of jet propulsion were applied for either subsonic or supersonic speeds, which had even been applied to helicopter flight. The fuel was piped into combustion chambers at the rotor blade tips where it exploded, whirling the blades around like a lawn sprinkler or pinwheel. As for rocket propulsion, the A-4 rocket had been put into large-scale production just as the war ended. It was 46 feet long, weighed over 24,000 pounds, and travelled at 230 miles. It rose 60 miles above the earth and had a maximum speed of 3,735 miles an hour – three times that of the earth's rotation at the equator. The secret of its supersonic speed, as we know today, lay in its rocket motor, which used liquid oxygen and alcohol for fuel. It was either radio-controlled or self-guided to its target by gyroscopic means. Since its speed was supersonic, it could not be heard before it struck.

Another German rocket in development was the A-9, weighing 29,000 pounds with wings giving it a flying range of 3,000 miles. It was manufactured at the famous Peenemuende army experiment station and achieved the unbelievable speed of 5,870 miles an hour. Wernher (later Werner) von Braun, who had headed the rocket programme, took American citizenship and went on to be chief architect of the Saturn V rocket, which propelled the US to the moon in 1967.

A long-range rocket-motored bomber that, as documents indicate, was never completed would have been capable of flying from Germany to New York in forty minutes. Pilot-guided from a pressurized cabin, it would have flown at an altitude of 154 miles. Launching was to be by catapult at 500 miles an hour allowing the ship to rise to its maximum altitude in four minutes. There, fuel exhausted, it would glide through the outer atmosphere, bearing down on its target. With 100 bombers of this type, the Germans hoped to destroy any city on earth within a few days.

The Germans even had devices for allowing pilots to leave supersonic planes during flight without destroying his parachute or having his head shorn off, by inventing an ejector seat that would fling the pilot clear instantaneously. The parachute was made of latticed ribbons, which would check his fall after the down-drag of his weight had closed all the holes.

Such revelations raised the question as to whether Germany had been adequately advanced in air, rocket, and missile research that, given a little more time, she might have won the war. Scientists and engineers declared that these revelations cut years from scientific investigations and there were still thousands of German patents to be screened.

The prototype of a fifty-knot hydrofoil, human torpedo and a unique two-man midget submarine was uncovered in Lübeck. In Kiel, which had been the centre of German naval inventions, they were able to retrieve plans for high-speed peroxide submarines and torpedoes; a large amount of new and ingenious weapons and parts of a Messerschmitt jet engine were retrieved from a train on the Danish border. The booty was fairly divided. The Type-17 submarine was shipped to America and the Type-18 went to Britain for trials.[6]

By 1947 German scientists were given employment contracts that included a clause forbidding them ever to talk about their experiences. By the end of summer, hundreds were employed across Britain and later a few were sent to Canada and Australia. Accordingly, many Germans would later be reunited with their families with the chance to settle and with adequate payment.

One of these 'key Germans' was Karl Doetsh, who had been discovered by British authorities in his home town of Bavaria, having cycled there from the aircraft base at Travemünde in northern Germany. He was a Flugbaumeister, an elite breed of German test pilots that brilliantly combined the expertise of a highly skilled trained engineer in aeronautical design with the flair of an experienced pilot – eagerly sought by all four Allies.

After being brought to England he was sent to the Royal Aircraft Establishment in Farnborough where he had difficulty in explaining to British engineers the advantages of the advanced aerodynamic constructions he had been working on during the war. Karl Doetsch was later put in charge of the Controls Division, where he worked on developing Concorde. He also became a Fellow of The Royal Aeronautical Society. In 1961 he returned to Germany to take up the position as Director of the Brunswick Institute of Technology.

11

BRITAIN AND GERMANY AFTER 1945

Throughout the centuries there has been a continual flow of Germans to Britain, along with a transfer of manpower, culture, learning and finance, through which both countries have greatly profited from the late Middle Ages onwards. Bearing in mind the history of both Britain and Germany, it appears paradoxical to human reasoning how and why these closely associated countries could slither into two unnecessary and devastating world wars, deemed the most destructive and unnatural events this planet has ever seen.

The Second World War – generated by the First World War and the Treaty of Versailles – had a devastating effect on Germany in every respect. The lack of democracy in the psyche of a nation resulted in the horrors of the Nazi dictatorship and the deaths of sixty million people, including the systematic elimination of six million Jews, causing a wave of animosity towards Germans for the following fifty years and, in some cases, beyond. The war caused not only worldwide destruction, but a rift between East and West that resulted in the growth of communism, the beginnings of the Cold War and changed the face of Europe. Almost half of the housing in Germany was estimated uninhabitable. Approximately twelve million displaced persons entered the country from Central and Eastern Europe, bringing further poverty and hunger without any prospect of improvement.

In contrast to the severe destruction of urban housing and lack of food, productive capital stock in Germany was in better shape than the victors had anticipated. Considerable wartime investment in industry combined with existing stock seemed a promising basis for quick recovery. However, Allied policies on German economic development were indecisive as to its future; whether to strip Germany of its potential development on one hand, or support cautious reconstruction on the other. On this question, Britain and America favoured a cautious rebuilding of the country while Russia's insistence upon introducing a communist system was the cause of a growing rift between East and West, and eventually led to the separation of East and West Germany. France, having regained the region of Alsace, played a minor role in the distribution of the booty.

The Nazi system had not only influenced the German political system significantly; it had also influenced how Germans thought about politics. There had been no history of a strong democratic tradition upon which the Germans could re-enter the political stage as an equal partner. The Weimar Republic, which had lasted less than twenty years from 1918 to 1933, had been the only democratic government in the country's history and had failed to protect it from the Nazi dictatorship. It is not surprising, therefore, that the democratisation of Germany was a principal aim of the allies.

Germany had to re-invent itself by fighting for acceptance among civilized nations.

Wilton Park, also known as the 'White House', which no longer exists. (Beaconsfield & District Historical Society).

Wilton Park in Buckinghamshire became a re-education centre for German prisoners of war considered capable of holding responsible positions in a new democratic Germany. Its founder was Heinz Koeppler, a German Jewish émigré who spent his life promoting open and frank discussion. In 1946 Köppler organised his first seminar in Wilton Park House in Buckinghamshire and immediate success led to a regular programme of courses on political, cultural and economic issues. Between 1946 and 1948, more than 4,000 Germans took part in the programme, many of whom would later gain influential positions in Germany.

Today Wilton Park is one of the world's leading centres for discussion of key international policy challenges.[1]

The single most important non-governmental effort to promote better understanding between Germany and Britain was the Deutsch-Englische Gesellschaft (DEG), founded on a private initiative of a small group around Lilo Milchsack (granddaughter of the German linguist Duden). First contact between Germans and the British occupation power were sought from 1945 onwards and still exist today, based on a mutual exchange of cultural and economic interests between both countries.

The first democratic activities took place in 1945 with the first elections in a small Bavarian village. Within months of the establishment of the occupational regimes, Germans were permitted to organise local, regional and state governments as well as regional and national parties. This was intended to enhance the federal structure in Germany where state governments were to play a significant role in balancing a future central government. Because of the speed of communist manifestation in the Eastern zone, the three Western Allies were eager to introduce democratic elections in the rest of the country and so by the middle of 1947 limited self-government had been established in all three Western zones.

In the British zone, which was generally assessed to be the best organised, many problems were magnified by the high population density, which made administration exceptionally difficult, especially regarding the feeding of the population, denazification and the dismantling of war and heavy industries. Also, tremendous war debts were straining the British economy, which was also suffering under the strains of supporting its colonies as well as Germany's recovery.

On 8 April 1948, the Marshall Plan (officially known as the European Recovery Programme, ERP) came into effect, named after the American Secretary of State George Marshall who implemented the plan. This was an American plan to give economic aid to Western Europe after the end of the Second World War, being convinced that a return of prosperity to Europe would prevent the spread of communism. The United States gave over $12 billion (approximately $120 billion in current dollar value as of June 2016) over a period of four years to rebuild war-devastated regions with the intention not only to modernise industry, but to remove trade barriers between the United States and European countries. The largest recipient of Marshall Plan money was the United Kingdom, which received about 26 per cent, followed by France with 18 per cent and West Germany with 11 per cent. Altogether, some eighteen European countries received Plan benefits. Russia refused to participate and blocked benefits to Eastern Bloc countries such as East Germany and Poland.

Throughout the following decades, Germany has rebuilt its economy and conveniently saved a great deal of money by paying less attention to military development thanks to earlier rearmament restrictions. It is governed as a federal republic, with power divided between states and voters, who have ultimate control of political issues.

It has been said that 'whenever post-war Britain built an Imperial War Museum, Germany built a new factory', which partly explains the different pace and success of German and British post-war economic recovery. The fact that Britain has always been able to dwell on its glorious past, the achievements and victories of its forefathers, has been in sharp contrast to Germany's shameful Third Reich. This prevents Germans from dwelling on any past heroic deeds, which are not well received by its neighbours and previous victors.

In his book *The English – A Portrait of a People,* Jeremy Paxman gives an ironic description of Germany and Britain's present situation:

Germany may be over-regulated and humourless, but it has at least reinvented itself as a prosperous, humane society after two world wars and Nazism, which is why Germans care what people think about them. The English have conspicuously failed to reinvent themselves. They just got poorer… but at least the English have the saving grace of being able to laugh at themselves.

NOTES

Chapter 1. Who Are The Germans?

1. *Anglo-Saxon Chronicle* at www.britannia.com.
2. Prof. Peter Donnelly; Welcome Trust Centre for Human Genetics, University of Oxford – studies summarised by Sarah Knapton, Science Editor of *The Daily Telegraph*, 18 March 2015.
3. Oxford Journals, *Medicine & Health & Science & Mathematics Molecular Biology and Evolution;* Volume 19, Issue 7; p. 1008–1021.
4. Prof. Dr Heinrich Härke, University of Reading Ur- und Frühgeschichte und Archäologie des Mittelalters.
5. www.historyfiles.co.uk/KingListsEurope/ScandinaviaAngeln.

Chapter 2. Early Trans-Migration

1. Panikos Panayi: *German Immigrants in Britain; Pre-Nineteenth Century.*
2. V. G. Kiernan: *Britons Old and New.*
3. V. G. Kiernan: *Britons Old and New:* also *Lappenburg, Urkundliche Geschichte des hansischen Stahlhofes zu London-Hamburg 1851* taken via Wikisource.
4. V. G. Kiernan: *Immigrants and Minorities in British Society; Britons Old and New.*
5. Prof. Rainer Postel, Bundeswehr Universität: *The Hanseatic League and its Decline.*
6. C. V. Wedgwood: *The Thirty Years War.*
7. Weltbild: *Die Deutsche Geschichte 1348–1855.*
8. Panikos Panayi: *German Migration to Britain,* p. 39.
9. Panikos Panayi: *German Immigrants in Britain – The Pre-Nineteenth Century Background,* pp. 12–13.
10. Panikos Panayi: *German Immigrants in Britain,* pp. 10–13.
11. Irish Palatine Association, Limerick, Ireland http://www.irishpalatines.org.
12. Panikos Panayi: *German Immigrants in Britain,* p. 13.
13. Margrit Schulte Beerbühl: *The Migration of German Merchants to England 1660–1800.*
14. Panikos Panayi: *German Migration to Britain,* p. 63.
15. Panikos Panayi: *German Immigrants in Britain During the 19th Century,* p. 67.
16. Margrit Schulte Beerbühl: *Commercial Networks, Transfer and Innovation – Migration and Transfer from Germany to Britain 1660–1914.*
17. Toni Pierenkemper, Richard H. Tilly: *The German Economy During the Nineteenth Century.*
18. Panikos Panayi: *German Immigrants in Britain,* p. 92.
19. Peter Towey: *Anglo-German Family History Society.*

Chapter 3. German Contribution Towards Britain's Economic Growth:

1. Margrit Schulte Beerbühl: *Commercial Networks, Transfer and Innovation; The Migration of German Merchants to England, 1660–1800.*
2. Hermann Kellenbenz: *German Immigrants in England.*
3. Colin Holmes: *Immigrants and Minorities in British Society.*
4. Margrit Schulte Beerbühl: *The Migration of German Merchants to England, 1660–1800.*
5. *Panikos Panayi: German Immigrants in Britain During the 19th Century,* p. 75.
6. Herbert Kaplan: *Russian Overseas Commerce with Great Britain.*
7. Margrit Schulte Beerbühl: *Staatsangehörigkeit und fremdes Know-How. Die deutschen Kaufleute im britischen Russlandhandel.*
8. Susan Duxbury-Neumann: *Little Germany: A History of Bradford's Germans.*
9. Margrit Schulte Beerbühl: *Commercial Networks, Transfer and Innovation – Migration and Transfer from Germany to Britain 1660–1914.*
10. *Dictionary of National Biography* 2004 – see also the career of Ambrose Gottfried Hanckwitt (1660–1741). A. E. Musson, Eric Robinson, *Science and Technology in the Industrial Revolution*, Manchester 1969 56f.
11. Colin Holmes: *Immigrants and Minorities in British Society*, p. 67.
12. The Baring Archive.
13. Information supplied by descendant, John Kennedy, Bradford.
14. Colin Holmes: *Immigrants and Minorities in British Society – German Immigrants in England.*
15. Taken from St George in the East Church, London – Sugar Refining.
16. Horst Rössler: *Germans from Hanover in the British Sugar Industry, 1750–1900.*
17. Panikos Panayi: *German Migrants and Culinary Transfer to Britain, c. 1850–1914.*
18. www.givethanksbakery.com/history/ – accessed 20.06.16.
19. Panikos Panayi: *German Migrants and Culinary Transfer to Britain, c. 1850–1914.*
20. Panikos Panayi: *German Immigrants in Britain*, p. 120 – *Major Occupations of Germans in England and Wales, 1861–1911.*
21. Panikos Panayi – De Montfort University; Stefan Manz – Aston University: *The Rise and Fall of Germans in the British Hospitality Industry, c. 1880–1920.*
22. Gambrinus Waltz: *German Lager Beer in Victorian and Edwardian London* by Ray Bailey and Jessica Boak – Taken from Boak and Bailey's Bier Blog – 'The best glass of lager in London', which goes on to mention another business – we guess was also German-owned and sold lager.
23. Kenneth James: *Escoffier, King of Chefs.*
24. Panikos Panayi: *German Migrants and Culinary Transfer to Britain 1850–1914.*
25. *Die deutsche Kolonie in London.* British Library 8139.k.9.
26. Panikos Panayi: *German Immigrants in Britain During the 19th Century*, p. 107.
27. Karl-Heinz Wüstner: *New Light on the German Pork Butchers in Britain.*
28. Newton Gerald: *Germans in Sheffield 1817–1918 German Life and Letters* Volume XLV, No. 1.
29. Panikos Panayi: *German Immigrants in Britain During the 19th Century*, p. 120.
30. Gibbons, Sue: *German Pork Butchers in Britain*, p. 11.
31. Karl-Heinz Wüstner: *New Light on the German Pork Butchers in Britain 1850–1950.*
32. With kind permission; Eileen Haffner: George Haffner (Foods) Ltd, Burnley.

Chapter 4. German Culture

1. F. Anne, M. R. Jarvis: *German Musicians in London c. 1750–1850.*
2. Panikos Panayi: *German Immigrants in Britain*, p. 20.

3. F. Anne, M. R. Jarvis: studies in local and regional history at Cambridge University into the community of German migrant musicians in London from 1750 to 1850.

4. F. Anne, M. R. Jarvis: *German Musicians in London 1750–1850*.

5. F. Anne, M. R. Jarvis: *German Musicians in London, 1750–1850*.

6. F. Anne, M. R. Jarvis: *German Musicians in London, 1750–1850*.

7. Euing Collection of letters and biographical papers at Glasgow University. 'Catherine Bisset' 84/22.

8. *Migration and Transfer from Germany to Britain 1660–1914*; see also F. Anne M. R. Jarvis: *German Musicians in London*.

9. Panikos Panayi: '*German Immigrants in Britain*, pp. 136/7.

10. Brand: *London Life*, p. 135.

11. Irene Hardach-Pinke – German Governesses in England – Prinz Albert und die Entwicklung der Bildung in England und Deutschland im 19. Jahrhundert: Franz Bosbach, William Filmer-Sankey, Hermann Hiery: Walter de Gruyter, 1 January 2000.

12. John Simkin – spartacus-educational.com/WmarionK – accessed 07.07.2016.

13. Gerlinde Röder-Bolton: *The Reception of Goethe's Work in the 19th Century*; and *Prince Albert and the Development of Education in the 19th Century*, pp. 213–224

Chapter 5. German Institutions

1. Panikos Panayi: *German Immigrants in Britain*, p. 81.

2. Reinhard Koselleck: *Preußen zwischen Reform und Revolution; Theodor Schieder: Vom Deutschen Bund zum Deutschen Reich 1815–1871*.

3. spartacus-educational.com/TUmarx – accessed 10.01.17.

4. Panikos Panayi: *German Immigrants in Britain – Ethnic Organisations*.

5. Panikos Panayi: *German Immigrants in Britain During the 19th Century*, p. 181.

6. Panikos Panayi: *German Immigrants in Britain During the 19th Century*, p. 184.

7. Susan Duxbury-Neumann: *Little Germany – A History of Bradford's Germans*.

8. wikipedia.org/wiki/National_Insurance_Act_1911 – accessed 10.01.2017.

9. Panikos Panayi: *German Immigrants in Britain During the 19th Century*, p. 158.

10. Panikos Panayi: *German Immigrants in Britain During the 19th Century*, p. 174.

11. London Metropolitan Archives: Information Leaflet Number 23; 'The German Community in London'.

12. Karl-Heinz Wüstner: *Die Deutsche Evangelische Kirche in Liverpool – ein Rückhalt für Seeleute und Einwanderer im 19. Jahrhundert*.

13. Panikos Panayi: *German Immigrants in Britain – Ethnic Organisations*, pp. 162–164.

14. Rabbi Dr Walter Rothschild, Berlin.

15. Panikos Panayi: *German Immigrants in Britain During the 19th Century*.

16. Todd M. Endelman: *The Jews of Britain, 1656 to 2000*.

17. Todd M. Endelman: *The Jews of Britain, 1656 to 2000*.

Chapter 6. German Ingenuity

1. Immigrants and Minorities in British Society, Hermann Kellenbenz: *German Immigrants in England*, pp. 71–72. Also – wikipedia.org/wiki/Friedrich_Accum.

2. University of Manchester Library Simon Engineering Group Archives 1860s–1970s. Also – wikipedia.org/wiki/Henry Gustav_Simon.

3. wikipedia.org/wiki/Ludwig_Mond.

4. Wilfried Feldenkirchen: *Werner von Siemens – Erfinder und International Unternehmer*.

5. wikipedia.org/wiki/Gottlieb_Daimler.

6. wikipedia.org/wiki/Carl_von_Linde.

Chapter 7. The Legacy of Prince Albert:

1. *BBC News Magazine*, 01.01.13.
2. Panikos Panayi: *German Immigrants in Britain – British Attitudes*, p. 230.
3. Jane Read: The dissemination of Friedrich Froebel's Kindergarten Ideology in Britain 1850-1900; chapter in *Prince Albert and the Development of Education in England and Germany in the 19th Century*.
4. Hermione Hobhouse: *The Contribution of Prince Albert to British Education* / Asa Briggs: *Politics and Reform – The British Universities* / Derek Beales: 'The Prince Consort and the University of Cambridge' – chapter in *Prince Albert and the Development of Education in England and Germany in the 19th Century*.
5. William Filmer-Sankey: 'E. R. Robson and the Influence of German School Planning in Later 19th Century England' – chapter in *Prince Albert and the Development of Education in England and Germany in the 19th Century*.
6. Mark Finlay: 'German-British Relations in the History of 19th Century Chemistry, Personal Friendship, Public Science and Private Enterprise' – chapter in *Prince Albert and the Development of Education in England and Germany in the 19th Century*.
7. www.royalcommission1851.org/archive.
8. Mark Finlay: *German-British Relations in the History of 19th Century Chemistry*.

Chapter 8. Hostility Towards Germans:

1. Hermann Kellenbenz: *German Immigrants in England – Immigrants and Minorities in British Society*, p. 64.
2. P. J. Nagle: *Prince Albert's Defence* / Martin: *Life of the Prince Consort*, vol.2 / Martin Kingsley, *The Triumph of Lord Palmerston* / Panikos Panayi: *German Immigrants in Britain 19th Century – British Attitudes*.
3. Michael T. Bass: *Street Music in the Metropolis*.
4. *Caterer and Hotel Proprietors Gazette*, 15 December 1890.
5. Panikos Panayi: *German Immigrants in Britain*, p. 227.
6. J. J. Findlay: *The Genesis of the German Clerk*.
7. Gregory Anderson: *German Clerks*, p. 204.
8. Gregory Anderson: *Victorian Clerks*, pp. 62–70.
9. John Ramsden: *Don't Mention the War*, pp. 49–50.
10. Weltbild: *Die Deutsche Geschichte, 1756–1944*.
11. Christopher Clark: *Wilhelm II: Die Herrschaft des letzten deutschen Kaisers'*.
12. William Le Queux: *Spies of the Kaiser: Plotting the Downfall of England*.
13. Christopher Clark: *Wilhelm II*.

Chapter 9. The Effects of War:

1. Christopher Clark: *Kaiser Wilhelm II: A Life in Power*.
2. The Lusitania Resource: www.rmslusitania.info.
3. Panikos Panayi: *Prisoners of Britain*, pp. 98–200.
4. Panikos Panayi: *Prisoners of Britain*, p. 204.
5. John Ramsden: *Don't Mention The War*, p. 143.
6. John Maynard Keynes: *The Economic Consequences of the Peace*.
7. Nikolaus Pevsner: *An Outline of European Architecture*.

Chapter 10. Victory and Defeat:

1. Sabine Lee: *Victory in Europe –Britain and Germany since 1945*, p. 9.
2. Tom Bower: *The Paperclip Conspiracy*, P. 5.
3. Tom Bower: *The Paperclip Conspiracy*, p. 82.

4. Tom Bower: *The Paperclip Conspiracy*, p. 178.
5. The American and British hunt for new technologies was described in the article 'German Secrets by the Thousands' by C. Lester Walker; *Harper's Magazine*, October 1946.
6. Tom Bower: *The Paperclip Conspiracy*.

Chapter 11. Britain and Germany After 1945:
1. The history of Wilton Park – www.wiltonpark.org.uk.

AUTHOR INFORMATION

Susan Duxbury-Neumann is married to a German and lives with her family on the German-Danish border. She was born in Baildon, West Yorkshire, a small moorland town on the outskirts of the industrial city of Bradford. Her first book – *Little Germany: A History of Bradford's Germans,* also published by Amberley – takes us back to the eighteenth and nineteenth centuries, when prosperous German wool merchants entered the country to settle in Bradford. They brought enormous wealth to the city, which became known as the 'wool capital of the world', and built their palatial warehouses in the part of Bradford known as 'Little Germany'.

Also by the same author, *Up the Gum Tree: In the Australian Outback*; the humorous and often poignant story of young German migrants who emigrated to Australia in the early 1960s.

Little Germany; A History of Bradford's Germans – ISBN: 978-1-4456-4962-7
Up the Gum Tree: In the Australian Outback – ISBN-13: 978-3-7347-6958-0

www.susanduxbury.com

BIBLIOGRAPHY

Bosbach, Franz (editor), Hermione Hobhouse, Irene Hardach-Pinke, Jane Read: *Prince Albert and the Development of Education in England and Germany in the 19*th *Century*. (Prince Albert Studies Band 18), published by K. G. Sauer, Munich.

Bower, Tom: *The Paperclip Conspiracy,* published by Michael Joseph Ltd.

Clark, Christopher: *Wilhelm II Die Herrschaft des letzten deutschen Kaisers*, published by Deutsche Verlags Anstalt.

Clark Christopher; *The Sleepwalkers – How Europe Went to War in 1914*, published by Harper Perennial.

Gibbons, Sue: *German Pork Butchers in Britain*, published by Anglo-German Family History Society Publications.

Holmes, Colin (editor), Hermann Kellenbenz: *Immigrants and Minorities in British Society*, published by George Allen & Unwin, London.

Lee, Sabine: *Victory in Europe – Britain and Germany Since 1945*, published by Pearson Education Ltd.

Manz, Stefan (editor), Margrit Schulte Beerbühl: *Migration and Transfer from Germany to Britain 1660–1914*; *Historical Relations and Comparisons* (Prince Albert Studies, Band 3), published by De Gruyter.

Panayi, Panikos: *German Immigrants in Britain During the 19th Century 1815–1914*, published by Berg Publishers Limited, Oxford UK.

Panayi, Panikos: *Prisoners of Britain*, published by Manchester University Press.

Ramsden, John: *Don't Mention The War*, published by Abacus.